THE EU & RUSSIA

The Promise of Partnership

by
John Pinder
&
Yuri Shishkov

THE FEDERAL TRUST

This book is published by the Federal Trust, whose aim is to enlighten public debate on federal issues of national, continental and global governance. It does this in the light of its statutes which state that it shall promote 'studies in the principles of international relations, international justice and supranational government.'

The Federal Trust conducts enquiries, promotes seminars and conferences and publishes reports and teaching materials. It is the UK member of the Trans-European Policy Studies Association (TEPSA), a grouping of fifteen think-tanks from member states of the European Union.

Up-to-date information about the Federal Trust can be found on the internet at www.fedtrust.co.uk

ISBN 1 903403 14 6

This book is the third title in the Federal Trust series *Europe's Eastern Borders*. The two previous volumes are available from the publisher: *The EU & Kaliningrad: Kaliningrad and the Impact of EU Enlargement* (2001, 0 903573 18 3) edited by James Baxendale, Stephen Dewar and David Gowan; and *The EU & Ukraine: Neighbours, Friends, Partners* (2002, 1 903403 18 9) edited by Ann Lewis.

The Federal Trust is a Registered Charity No. 272241

Dean Bradley House, 52 Horseferry Road,

London SW1P 2AF

Company Limited by Guarantee No.1269848

Marketing and Distribution by Kogan Page Ltd

Printed by JW Arrowsmith

Contents

About the authors

John Pinder OBE has written extensively on the European Union and on its place in the world, including Russia and Eastern Europe in particular. His books include *The European Union and Eastern Europe* (1991), *The Building of the European Union* (1998) and *The European Union: A Very Short Introduction* (2001). He was the Director of the Policy Studies Institute (1964-85), Visiting Professor at the College of Europe (1970-99) and is Chairman of the Federal Trust.

Professor Yuri Shishkov is the head of the section on economic globalisation and regional integration at the Institute of World Economy and International Relations in Moscow. He is the author of seven books on international economy and regional integration and of many articles on relations between Russia and the EU, as well as on Russian external economic strategy. He and Pinder have already co-operated on a number of projects regarding relations between the EU and Russia.

Foreword

I am deeply grateful to Yuri Shishkov for his co-operation in the writing of this book. The promise of our own partnership dates from the 1970s, when his work expressed his understanding and appreciation of the European Community in circumstances that were very far from easy for him. By the end of the century, I thought the time was ripe for a study of partnership between the European Union and Russia that would show how its present state and future potential look to a sympathetic observer from each of the two sides; and this book is the result.

While the general intention is to contribute to knowledge about how the EU-Russia partnership now stands, the book also has the specific aim of suggesting ways in which the Union's policies could be developed to the benefit of both the parties. My chapters are therefore more policy-oriented than Shishkov's. His aim is rather to assess the present condition of Russia, analysing the problems that have made the transition to pluralist democracy and market economy particularly difficult, showing how much has nevertheless been achieved and explaining why so many among the elite who make or influence Russian policy set store by the promise of partnership with the Union: all of which has to be understood if EU policies are to be soundly based. My chapters seek to show how the Union's policies towards Russia have developed; how they have been constrained by weaknesses in its institutions and by Member States' perceptions of their own interests; in what respects the further development of the partnership could be beneficial; and how it could be accomplished.

While we have sought to avoid unnecessary overlaps between our texts, we have both dealt with some similar material in order to give readers a flavour of the different approaches or to show what is given greater salience by one side or the other. We would have liked to give more time to obtaining the advice of other observers and practitioners. But the events of 11 September 2001 made the theme so actual and urgent as to tilt the scales towards rapid publication. I am therefore all the more grateful to those who gave their advice on parts of the text or helped us in other ways, including Sir Rodric Braithwaite, Joly Dixon, Paola Gosparini, David Gowan, Axelle Nicaise, Ernst Piehl, Baron Snoy, Ivan Szegari and Simon Usherwood. Special thanks are due to Dusan Jakovljevic at the Federal Trust for his commitment to getting the book published as fast as possible.

John Pinder
December 2001

Preface

Christopher Patten
The EU Commissioner for
External Relations

The Federal Trust is to be congratulated on producing such a comprehensive insight into the complexities of relations between the European Union and Russia under President Putin. John Pinder and Yuri Shishkov offer complementary perspectives based on an impressive depth of knowledge from both sides of the relationship.

Enlargement of the EU to the East opens a new chapter in relations with Russia just as Russia's own situation is evolving more quickly than at any moment since the fall of the Berlin wall. This timely new book provides an accessible and fresh account of a fascinating subject.

INTRODUCTION

John Pinder

In October 1999, not long after his nomination as High Representative for the European Union's common foreign and security policy, Javier Solana said that to develop the partnership with Russia was 'the most important, the most urgent and the most challenging task that the Union faces at the beginning of the twenty first century.'[1]

It is indeed a vital task. For the European Union, Russia is an essential source of energy supplies as well as a potentially important market with a rapidly growing economy. For Russia, the Union is the biggest trade partner and potential source of investments and up-to-date technology. To complete the transition to a market economy and stable democracy is Russia's declared aim; and the Union's interest is to give what help an outsider usefully can to assist the process, because even if Russian democracy remains somewhat different from that of most other European countries, perhaps more 'guided' or 'manipulated' from above,[2] the result will be good both for Russia and for Europe as a whole.

A successful partnership will also contribute much to European security not, as Solana put it, 'for fear of a major war', but because Russia and the Union together could do much to deal with common problems such as organised crime, trafficking in drugs and people, nuclear or other environmental hazards and conflicts on the peripheries of Europe. The events of 11 September 2001 have provided the most powerful demonstration possible of the need to give the fight against terrorism a prominent place in that list.

The partnership may also be seen as a major element in a policy for the Union of forging partnerships with other major powers as a basis for a sound and stable world order.

But before we consider how a strong partnership may be built, it is useful to recall why its development is such a difficult process.

A difficult learning process for both Russia and the Union

Until the 1980s, relations between the European Community and the Soviet Union were frozen in the Cold War. It was not until 1985, when Mikhail Gorbachev became Secretary General of the Communist Party of the Soviet Union, that defreezing of the relationship began, together with the disintegration of the Soviet system. The Russian Federation, constituted in 1991, has had to adjust to an altogether new relationship with the other states of the former Soviet Union and with those of Central and Eastern Europe that had been subject to Soviet domination; and Russia has at the same time been undergoing the transition from the Soviet system towards a market economy and pluralist democracy. All this has been an intensely difficult learning process for the Russians; and it has also been hard for the EU and its member states to understand how to relate to a Russia in the process of such tectonic change.

The EU, with the complexity of its institutions and of their relationship with the member states, is likewise hard for Russians to understand. Nor is it that easy for most people within the Union; and the difficulty for both sides has been compounded by the period of rapid change in the Union that began, like the end of the Cold War, in the 1980s.

Soon after Jacques Delors became President of the European Commission in 1985, only a few weeks before Gorbachev became Secretary General of the Soviet Union's Communist Party, he initiated a process of radical change in the Community. The first fruits were the Single European Act and the single market programme, together with the practice of majority voting for most decisions in the Council of Ministers. Gorbachev's withdrawal of the Soviet Union from Central and Eastern Europe was the catalyst for the next phase of change, because one of the conditions of German unification in October 1990 was agreement between France and Germany to consolidate the Community by promoting monetary union and a common foreign and security policy; and this led to the Maastricht Treaty which, together with the Amsterdam Treaty, gave what was henceforth called the European Union its powers in these fields as well as some others such as internal security, and also strengthened the European Parliament and extended the scope for majority voting in the Council.

The EU has since been learning how to use these new powers and institutions: an enormously complicated task of integration, in parallel with that of Russia's transition from the disintegrated Soviet system, which itself has given the EU another new and demanding task: the negotiations for accession of ten Central and East European countries. This comprehensive learning process has absorbed time and energy that could have been devoted to the relationship with Russia.

The prospect of EU enlargement affects Russia in other ways. To the common frontier between the EU and Russia that resulted from Finnish accession in 1995 will be added those with Estonia and Latvia when they accede; and Russia's exclave, Kaliningrad, borders with Poland and Lithuania, thus making it an EU enclave after they join. Enlargement will also raise the EU's share of Russia's trade to more than one-half; and while it may enhance the stability of Russia's political relations with Central and East European countries, it will doubtless engender political and economic problems too.

So we should not be surprised if building a partnership between the EU and Russia is a difficult task. The partnership between the European Union and the United States is, after all, not without its problems, despite half a century of experience in the relationship between two such similar systems. But this book has been written in the conviction that a successful partnership between the EU and Russia would be a great prize, both for its two participants and for the wider world.

The book is therefore oriented towards policies, particularly on the part of the EU, that might help to strengthen the partnership. The first chapter examines the Union's policies in the economic field where most of its instruments and institutions are comparatively well tried and tested and where the intention is not only to look after its shorter-term interests but also to advance its longer-term interest of a successful Russian transition. The analysis by Professor Shishkov in chapter two of the problems of the economic transition provides an indication as to how far the Union's policies respond to them. Chapter three, also by Shishkov, outlines Russia's policies in relation to the Union and the thinking and attitudes that underlie them. Chapter four considers the Union's Common Strategy on Russia, which brings together the external economic policies with other elements of the common foreign and security policy. As well as examining problems and policies as they have existed up to now, it suggests ways of strengthening the policies not only in the context of the Union's capacity based on its present instruments and structures, but also with reforms designed to enhance its capacity. Chapter 5 concludes by bringing together the main suggestions for the EU's policies towards Russia and for reform of the Union in order to make the policies effective.

The reader should be warned that the thrust of the suggested reforms stems from a profound conviction that 'in today's interdependent world, pooling sovereignty, when we choose to, is the way to strengthen sovereignty, not lose it.'[3] The Union can do useful things as it stands at present. But without such reforms, it cannot play the part it should in giving such great projects as partnership with Russia the best prospect of success.

Chapter 1:
The Union's Economic
Policies towards Russia

John Pinder

Already in the 1960s the European Community, with its common external tariff and commercial policy, became a trading power able to hold its own with the United States in international trade negotiations. But when it came to negotiate on trade with the Soviet Union's command economy, the Community was not able to apply its weight to achieve a significant result. It was not willing to play the Soviet game of state-led quantitative barter; nor did it find a way to engage the Soviet Union in meaningful negotiations such as those on tariffs among market economies. The bulk of its imports from the Soviet Union were in any case raw materials, on which the Community imposed no tariffs or other restrictions, so Soviet negotiators had no significant demands that the Community could satisfy; and although Central and East European countries could benefit from the reduction of tariffs and quotas on their exports of manufactures and agricultural products, the Soviet Union constrained the scope of their negotiations with the Community, and such negotiations as were allowed faced the difficulty of finding genuine reciprocity between the different systems.[4]

As Gorbachev relaxed the constraints on Central and East European countries, the Community began to conclude Trade and Co-operation Agreements with them: first with Hungary and Czechoslovakia in 1988, with Poland in 1989, then in December of that year with the Soviet Union itself. With these, the Community guaranteed most-favoured-nation tariffs, which it had already granted de facto, and reduced the scope of quantitative restrictions. There was also provision for 'Co-operation' in a number of fields, which was given substance when the Community launched its Phare programme of technical assistance for Central and East Europeans in 1990 and Tacis for Russia and the rest of the Commonwealth of Independent States (CIS) in 1991. Then, responding to the process of transition to market economies, the Community began in 1990 to negotiate association agreements with Central and East European countries; and Partnership and Co-operation Agreements (PCAs) with CIS countries followed, the first of which, with Russia, was signed in 1994.[5]

The PCA provided a stronger framework for trade and co-operation and more developed institutions than the trade and co-operation agreements. The idea of creating 'the necessary conditions for the future establishment of a free trade area' with the Community was introduced, but without a date or a programme for moving towards it. A large number of fields were listed for co-operation, which was bolstered by an expanded Tacis programme. The institutions are a Co-operation Council, comprising ministers from both parties and members of the European Commission; a Co-operation Committee of senior officials, which formed nine sub-committees to deal with particular aspects; and a Parliamentary Co-operation Committee of members of the Russian Parliament and the European Parliament. The agreements are to apply for ten years in the first instance then to be renewed automatically each year unless either party gives six months notice to terminate them.

Although signed in June 1994, the PCA with Russia did not enter into force until December 1997, because the European Union delayed it as a consequence of the first Chechen war. So the Co-operation Council first met only in January 1998, followed by the Co-operation Committee in April. Although the Union devised an interim agreement under which the provisions on trade would apply meanwhile, valuable time was lost in learning to work together within the institutions. Chapter four returns to the question of the Union's reaction to the Chechen wars.

The PCA has had less content than the Europe Agreements that associate the Central and East European states with the Union, partly because the latter contain timetables for establishing free trade areas and have become antechambers for accession to the Union. Although providing the necessary framework for developing the trade relationship, moreover, the implementation of the PCA has been judged disappointingly complex and bureaucratic, with papers passed up and down between the Co-operation Council, the Co-operation Committee and the sub-committees: 'a triumph of process over substance'.[6] The six-monthly Summits in which the Russian President and Prime Minister meet the President-in-Office of the European Council, together with the Commissioner responsible for external relations and the EU's High Representative for the common foreign and security policy, have been more productive, with better results since Vladimir Putin became President of the Russian Federation in May 2000. But although these have tended to focus on questions of foreign and security policy, the economic field has so far remained the most substantial part of the relationship.

Trade

Trade with the Union accounts for just over one-third of Russia's total external trade. While the Russian share of the Union's trade is only 3-4 per cent, reflecting the fact that its trade with the rest of the world is some ten times as big as Russia's, Russia is a qualitatively important trading partner because it is a reliable source of a large share of the Union's imports of energy supplies.

Table 1.1: EU exports to Russia, 2000

	$ billion
foodstuffs	1.2
beverages and tobacco	0.3
chemicals	2.2
paper and manufactures	0.4
textiles	0.3
iron and steel, incl. manufactures	0.5
machinery	3.5
road vehicles, tractors and other transport equipment	0.5
scientific instruments	0.6
other	1.9
total	**11.4**

Source: *EIU Country Profile: Russia 2001*, The Economist Intelligence Unit.

Some specific irritants have faced exporters to Russia, such as over-enthusiastic banning of meat imports and taxation of imports of alcoholic beverages and of airlines flying over the country. But as Shishkov recounts in chapter two, there has been extensive liberalisation of imports; and the principal problem, apart from Russia's profound recession, has been the difficulty presented by the inadequate rule of law. Since world trade has become increasingly associated with foreign direct investment, the failings of corporate governance in Russia, with the consequent deterrence of foreign investment, have been a further constraint on the development of trade.

Meanwhile Russian supplies of oil and gas will remain of strategic importance to the Union for a long time to come. Two-fifths of the EU's imports of gas, around 100 million tons of oil equivalent, come from Russia and around one-eighth of its imports of oil. The European Commission has initiated proposals for a twenty-year 'energy partnership' between the EU and Russia, which were launched at the EU-Russia Summit in Paris in October 2000, envisaging investments and technology transfer linked with long-term contracts that would provide for up to a doubling of imports of gas and substantial increases in imports of oil and electricity.[7] While the extraction and transport of gas and oil on this scale involves formidable costs and technical skills, a more immediate problem has been the lack of confidence in the reliability of key Russian enterprises as investment partners, following unfortunate experiences on the part of western firms investing in Russia. The Commission has, however, pointed out that the continuity of energy supplies from Russia, and formerly the Soviet Union, over the past quarter of a century has been 'testimony to an exemplary stability';[8] and detailed proposals were agreed at the EU-Russia Summit in October 2001 to carry forward the establishment of an 'energy partnership', including measures to assure western companies that investment in Russia will be sufficiently safe.[9] Exxon's announcement that it would, together with Japanese, Indian and Russian partners, proceed with the Sakhalin 1 project involving an investment of $12 billion was a very positive sign. This is by far the largest foreign investment project in Russia so far; and big investments on the part of other major oil companies, including Shell and Total, may well follow.[10]

Table 1.2: EU imports from Russia, 2000

	$ billion
crude petroleum	8.8
gas	8.2
other mineral fuels	5.8
wood, pulp, paper and manufactures	1.3
chemicals	1.5
iron and steel and manufactures	1.3
copper and manufactures	1.1
nickel and manufactures	1.6
aluminium and manufactures	1.5
machinery	0.9
transport equipment	0.2
other	1.9
total	**34.1**

Source: *EIU Country Profile: Russia 2001*, The Economist Intelligence Unit.

Such an expansion of gas and oil exports could raise the share of mineral fuels in total Russian exports to two-thirds or more, making it the more important for Russia to increase other exports by making them competitive in world markets. The EU's tariffs are generally low and Russia is accorded preferences. Most tariffs of Central and East European countries are at present higher, so Russian exports will benefit when they join. But there are still sectors in which the EU is protectionist. Agriculture is of course one; and in so far as Russia can provide agricultural products, they are seriously impeded. Though most quotas have been abolished, they still apply to imports of steel; and the Union does not yet treat Russia as a market economy in applying its anti-dumping policy, thus, as Shishkov points out, placing Russian exporters at a disadvantage. But it is more generally non-tariff barriers such as differing standards and regulations that are likely to restrict the growth of trade.

The difference between Russian and Union standards and regulations will become increasingly problematic for Russian exports of manufactures and services that would be competitive in other respects, particularly as they are being adopted by the prospective Central and East European member states which remain significant markets for Russian products and formerly applied the Soviet versions. Having enacted its own rules following complicated negotiations among the member states, the Union is not likely to modify them. So Article 55 of the PCA, on legal co-operation, commits the Russian Federation to endeavour to ensure that its legislation becomes gradually compatible with that of the Union, 'including technical rules and standards.' Russia's Medium-term Strategy for relations with the Union states that Russia will pursue 'approximation and harmonisation with the EU legislation in areas of the most active EU-Russia co-operation.'[11] Senior officials have been more forthcoming, recognising that Russia must 'upgrade to EU standards.'[12] But that is a hard task and help is needed from the Tacis programme.

Meanwhile Russia is seeking to join the World Trade Organisation in order to secure the best possible access to world markets. The aim has been reported as membership in 2003 or 2004, followed by a substantial transitional period before all conditions required of a completed market economy will have been satisfied. While doubts have been expressed whether membership will be possible so soon, the Union, in its Common Strategy on Russia, has affirmed its readiness 'to maintain, and if appropriate, enhance' its support for Russian efforts to meet the requirements for accession to the WTO 'at the earliest possible date'; and at the Summit in October 2001 both parties agreed to speed up the process of negotiating terms for accession.[13]

Russia has also expressed the wish to consider, 'with experts of the European Union [...] availability of conditions for opening negotiations' on establishing the free trade area envisaged in the PCA.[14] The Union's policy has been to postpone further discussion on the subject until Russia has joined the WTO. This is logical, in that the conditions are among those that would have to be satisfied for the establishment of a free trade area, which is a more distant prospect. But given the importance of building the partnership with Russia, the concept of a 'Common European Economic Area' has been devised, which may be seen as a step in the direction of the more distant aim. The EU-Russia Summit of October 2001 decided to establish a High-Level Group to elaborate the concept, considering opportunities for 'greater integration and legislative approximation'; and an energy partnership would also be seen as part of it.[15] The CEEA could, if enough substance is put into it, be a significant element in the developing partnership between the EU and Russia, helping the Russians to create a normal European-type market economy.

Tacis

The Union has a particular interest in co-operation in areas of 'established Russian expertise' such as science, aircraft, space and energy.[16] But in most of the others among over thirty areas listed in the PCA's articles on co-operation, its interest is the more general one of helping Russia to develop a well-functioning market economy; and here, the co-operation can have a great deal more substance if it is based on financially supported assistance, i.e. on the Tacis programme of 'Technical Assistance to the Commonwealth of Independent States'. Tacis is, indeed, what Javier Solana called 'our flagship' in the Union's action to support, as the PCA put it, 'Russian efforts to consolidate its democracy and to develop its economy and to complete the transition into a market economy'.[17]

After the provision of emergency aid, mainly food, during the early phase of dismantling the Soviet system, the Union launched the Tacis programme, focused on restructuring to form competitive enterprises for a viable market economy. Experience showed, however, that this policy would not be sufficiently effective without the legal, administrative and political framework for such an economy, which in Russia was still seriously deficient. So the objective of the programme, initially confined to 'the transition to a market economy', was broadened by stages through the 1990s and became, by the end of the decade, 'to promote the transition to a market economy and to reinforce democracy and the rule of law.'[18] It has become clear that success with these wider objectives is a condition of successful restructuring and macroeconomic policies; and it also accords with the aim, shared by both Russia and the Union, of developing a partnership for the long term.

The principal way of transmitting assistance through the 1990s has been to send consultants from the Union to give the Russians advice. The independent report evaluating Tacis, produced for the European Commission in January 2000, was surely right to conclude that whereas the advice of such consultants had generally been to apply 'the right way' to deal with a problem in a normally functioning market economy, this was not usually the best way in Russian conditions, which requires understanding of what Russians need to complete their transition.[19] The result has too often been reports that were not implemented, either because they were not appropriate, or because the

Russians, feeling no sense of 'ownership', did not feel motivated to implement them. Successful assistance needs to be accompanied by plenty of dialogue to build understanding and trust, which takes time and is, as far as possible, provided by people who already have an understanding of Russian conditions. The number of people in the Union who really know how to deal with Russian problems is still very limited.[20] So it is understandable that consultants' advice has not been as useful as could be desired.

The Commission has been acting along the lines indicated in the Evaluation Report. The 'Tacis Indicative Programme 2000-2003' envisages 'an intensified dialogue-driven approach' and emphasises 'the creation of long-term and sustainable partnerships between EU and Russian operators [...] going beyond the scope of individual projects.' There is to be wider use of local experts in support of EU expertise, and support of links such as exchanges and twinning is to be widespread among both the public and the private sectors, including the civil society.[21]

This policy is, in addition to the more immediate benefits for Russia's transition, an essential investment in the human infrastructure that is required for building a long-term partnership. It needs to be carried forward consistently and to be based on a budget that reflects the importance of the objective.

The total allocations for all Tacis programmes for Russia in the 1990s averaged over €200 million a year:[22] a substantial sum, but less than one-fifth as much per head of population as the Phare allocations for Central and Eastern Europe. About one-third of the total was Russia's estimated share of the allocations for the part of the Tacis budget that refers to the CIS as a whole, of which the largest items were nuclear safety and regional programmes. Of the other two-thirds, which was allocated specifically to Russia, the largest items were a group of specific sectors (agriculture, energy, transport and telecommunications), restructuring in the private sector, human resources development and public administration, policy advice and small project programmes. Shishkov observes that Tacis has on the whole been well received in Russia.

In reaction against the second Chechen war, the specific allocation for

Russia was cut from €140 million in 1998 to €92 million in 1999, with a shift towards focusing on education, the rule of law, democracy and civil society development; and there was only a modest increase to €98 million for 2000. While the effect on actual expenditure was less dramatic, can this really be the best way to contribute towards raising the standards of human rights in the Russian Federation, which is not likely to be achieved without a successful transition in the economy as well as the polity? Russia's share of the allocations for programmes covering the CIS as a whole, of which nuclear safety remained the largest, rose however from €80 million in 1999 to €100 million in 2000. At the end of 1998, Russia was also awarded an EU food aid programme of €470 million to help ensure that food was available to those in need.

Table 1.3: Tacis allocations for Russia, 1998-2000

	€ million		
	1998	1999	2000
institutional, legal and administrative reform	30	15	28
private sector support and economic development	32	18	14
alleviation of social consequences of transition	3	5	6
developments of infrastructure networks	20	11	0
environmental protection, natural resources management	10	8	4
rural economic development	9	5	0
policy advice, small projects programmes	28	23	39
other	10	8	7
total	·140	92	98

Source: European Commission.

The small projects programmes comprise clusters of projects generally costing up to €2 million each which, having been found more effective than the large ones in securing advice appropriate for Russian conditions and the commitment of the Russian partner, have been accorded the largest allocation. They include a Managers' Training Programme, which the Evaluation Report found had 'created a widespread Russian capacity to assist enterprises on a sustainable market basis'; institution building; and support for investments of small and medium enterprises and municipal authorities.[23] The broad priorities reflected in the other main headings shown in the table apply to the smaller as to the larger projects. The distinctive feature is the method of delivery specific to the smaller ones, found to be more effective in establishing durable relationships and a greater sense of Russian ownership. The Bistro scheme, under which decisions are taken quickly by the Union's delegation in Moscow, was a response to the delays of sometimes up to a year and a half in authorising projects, which as Shishkov notes have been irksome for Russians. Chris Patten, the Commissioner for external relations, has however initiated a process of further decentralising decision-taking to the Union's delegations in countries receiving assistance; and many of the projects for Russia are now authorised by the delegation in Moscow.

The Tempus programme, which finances collaborative projects between institutions of higher education in the partner country and two or more member states, based on a 'partnership of equals' in the vital fields of education and training, has had a beneficial impact.[24] Russians appreciate it. The total budget of some €80 million in the period 1993-2000 financed over 300 projects involving over 120 universities. Each partner country chooses the share of its total Tacis budget that is to go to Tempus and Russia has chosen to increase its share considerably, so that more than a hundred projects were under way in 2001. The major fields are economics, university management, EU languages and social sciences; and a programme of student mobility projects was recently initiated.[25]

Reflecting impatience about the scale of this compared with the historic importance of building the partnership with Russia, a massive exchange programme has been suggested, along the lines of the Socrates-Erasmus programme of student exchanges within the Union, together with periods in the West for 'tens of thousands' of business managers, professionals, civil servants and people working in non-governmental organisations, and with some movement of such people from the Union to Russia.[26] While such exchanges have to respect limits to the capacity of both sides to handle them successfully, this should be developed over time in the direction suggested. As a former British ambassador to Moscow has put it, the flow of people will come from 'the new middle class that began to emerge in the past decade, who will bring about the profound changes in attitudes, practices, and institutions that Russia needs';[27] and, it may be added, these are people who will be decisive in building the partnership with the European Union. The relatively modest finance required should not be the constraint.

The objectives of the other large programme, on institutional, legal and administrative reform, include strengthening the rule of law and improving corporate governance together with the business climate; and the main projects include tax reform, state budget reform, control of public expenditure, reform of the banking system and the Policy Advice Programme. These reflect a sensible judgement as to what Russia needs in developing the framework for its market economy and democratic polity. In the perspective of the EU-Russia partnership, the Policy Advice Programme is of particular interest, having a useful track record and greater potential for the relationship.

The Evaluation Report found Tacis to have been the main source of external policy advice and training in public administration for Russian federal ministries and regional authorities. So Tacis is well placed to help them develop the administrative and legislative framework that Russia needs and at the same time to strengthen the EU-Russia partnership. But it was suggested that Tacis consultants could do more to secure Russian commitment to implement their proposals, for example by sharper focus on the problems of implementation and by working with Russian consultants from the outset of a project. While steps are being taken to put these suggestions into practice, it was also suggested that, with success at the regional and ministerial levels, the programme could reach to the top level of government.[28] This would be highly significant for the future of the partnership. It would surely be worthwhile to attract the most highly qualified people to develop this field of work.

The provision of advice through the Tacis programme, as through those of the member states, would indeed justify a commitment to attract the most suitable people, provide any desirable further training for them and retain their services to enable them to form long-term relationships with Russian institutions and people with whom they work. The Commission itself has been understaffed and overloaded for its work on Tacis. While the situation has improved, it is important that the Commission should not be short of the necessary human resources. The programme should moreover have the financial as well as human resources that measure up to the significance of the task.

Foreign direct investment

Direct investment by foreign companies is the most effective way to transmit technology, managerial and entrepreneurial skills. Direct investors in emerging market economies can, for their part, benefit from low costs, high growth and getting in on the ground floor of a future mature market economy. They are increasingly attracted to Central and East European countries that are due to join the Union before long. Thus direct investment in Poland rose in 2000 to around $10 billion. For Russia, the annual average from 1994 to 1996 was less than $2 billion. It rose to average $4.4 billion in 1997-2000,[29] and the rate of inflow increased again in the first half of 2001, though it appears that a substantial part of it during the past couple of years has been returning Russian capital.

While the prospect of Russian membership of the Union is absent and that of a free trade area still distant, this is nevertheless a striking discrepancy; and the reason has been the poor framework and climate for investors. As the European Bank of Reconstruction and Development (EBRD) has put it, 'arbitrary and highly discretionary application of the legal and regulatory rules, paired with corruption, has been the fundamental flaw in the investment climate';[30] and *The Economist* has expressed the contribution of some Russians to one aspect of this state of affairs more bluntly: 'Russian bosses siphon cash from the companies they run to the companies they own.'[31] The EBRD and others have identified the elements required to make Russia safe for the foreign investor: the rule of law, including contract enforcement, clear and enforceable company law, together with independent and effective legal institutions; proper company governance, including financial transparency and protection of shareholders; and less corruption. A survey of three thousand companies showed Russia, with the cost to companies of corruption at 4.1 per cent of revenues in 1999, to be closer to the average of 3.3 per cent for Central and East European countries than to that of 5.7 per cent for countries of the CIS; and for big companies it was considerably less than for small ones.[32] It is evidently not here that the big difference between Russia and some of the Central and East European countries lies. It is, rather, in risks of the type described so succinctly by *The Economist*, offsetting the great growth potential.

A distinct improvement in the standards of corporate governance, at least in some of the largest enterprises, has more recently been observed, since their owners have come to realise the potential gains for shareholder value.[33] The Russian government moreover adopted, in July 2000, reforms designed to improve the climate for investment. The EBRD, with its mission to promote healthy development of the private sector backed by its financial muscle, can also exert a substantial influence for better corporate governance.

The EBRD

The EBRD was founded in 1990 on the initiative of the European Union, with the majority of its shares owned by the member states, to help the development of transition economies, mainly in their private sectors: specifically 'to foster the transition towards open-market oriented economies and to promote private and entrepreneurial initiative' in countries 'committed to applying the principles of multi-party democracy, pluralism and market economies'. Successful transition was evidently seen as a public good of such significance to the member states and other subscribing countries, including the US, as to justify investing public money before private investors were ready to bear the full risk. But the EBRD is a bank, subject to criticism if the risk turns out to be too costly; and it was indeed criticised when several projects among its Russian portfolio suffered particularly heavy losses associated with Russia's financial crisis of August 1998. But a large part of these losses have since been recovered; and the EBRD's government shareholders clearly accept that the risk of investing in Russia is worth taking, as they have agreed that, with less help required for private investment in the Central and East European countries which will before long become members of the Union, the Bank should shift its emphasis towards investment in the CIS.

The Bank's President, Jean Lemierre, was therefore able to say in April 2001 that the 1998 crisis had shown how much need there was for public investment when private investors had turned away.[34] Through the 1990s up to the end of the decade, the Bank had committed €3.5 billion to its Russian portfolio, four-fifths in the private sector. Its commitments in 2000 were at the enhanced rate of €579 million; for 2001 they are expected to amount to some €700 million and from 2002 onwards to around €1 billion a year. Thus the EBRD has taken the lead in renewing the access of Russia's private sector to international sources of capital.[35]

The Bank will at the same time do what it can to promote a positive climate for investment, pursuing its policy of priority for objectives of corporate governance such as transparency and shareholders' rights; and it gives special mention to the energy sector, reflecting its importance and the problems of corporate governance that have arisen there.[36]

This policy has already borne some fruit. The biggest Russian oil company, Lukoil, sought $150 million of EBRD finance, regarding it among other things as an international 'stamp of approval'. One matter that preoccupied the Bank was, however, the relationship between Lukoil and Reforma, a company based in Cyprus which had bought a stake of 9 per cent in Lukoil at what was seen as a low price and which was 'believed by some' to be linked to the company's executives.[37] The Bank insisted that Lukoil produce accounts to accord with international accounting standards and should in particular disclose its ownership structure. By March 2001, Lukoil had done so and the Bank approved its investment.

This was a significant achievement. The discussions of a strategic EU-Russia energy partnership cannot succeed unless western oil companies are prepared to invest in it. Don Evans, the US Commerce Secretary, has said that big investments in energy such as an oil pipeline from Azerbaijan and one for conveying gas from Sakhalin to Japan would be crucial in convincing American investors to return to Russia;[38] and the decision of Exxon and partners to proceed with a massive investment for oil production based on Sakhalin is very encouraging. Decisions to provide capital for the vast projects involved in the EU-Russia discussions, including two pipelines from North-West Russia to the Union, will likewise help to determine the future of foreign direct investment in Russia. The EBRD has stressed the need to raise corporate standards of monopolies in the gas and power sectors in particular;[39] and while the Bank made some progress with Lukoil, it has not yet had similar success with Gazprom, which has sought an investment of $250 million. Questions have been asked about the Florida-based company, Itera, which was 'widely suspected' of having links with Gazprom's management analogous to those that raised concern about the relationship between Lukoil and Reforma.[40] The Bank has not yet been satisfied by the response; but the replacement of Gazprom's head by one of Putin's own men should lead to a change of the company's policy, if its significance for the future of the Russian economy is properly understood.

The EBRD also contributes to Russian development with respect to small and medium enterprises, the environment and the regions, as well as other fields such as infrastructure and the financial sector. It places its investments in SMEs through institutions such as the Russian Small Business Fund and Regional Venture Funds. By August 2001 it had disbursed $647 million resulting in loans to some 61,000 businesses; and its wider aims were to work for a better legislative, administrative and tax environment for SMEs as well as institutions providing services and finance.[41] The Bank's statutes require it to promote, in all its activities, 'environmentally sound and sustainable development.' It aims to promote energy efficiency, waste reduction, cleaner technologies and renewable resources; it incorporates Environmental Action Plans in appropriate legal documentation; and it is to provide training for environmental consultants in a number of cities to help them to provide services for its clients.[42] The Bank has also selected priority regions for its attention, including St Petersburg, Novgorod, Perm, Samara and Vologda.[43]

Since the meeting of the European Council under Swedish Presidency in March 2001, the European Investment Bank has been authorised to allocate €100 million for Russian projects with environmental benefits, though without the EBRD's special focus on investing in the private sector; and at the end of that month a Memorandum of Understanding was signed for co-operation between the European Community, the EBRD and the World Bank. The latter has, since the Russian financial crisis of 1998 which wiped out the savings of large numbers of Russians and turned many of them against liberal market policies, shifted the emphasis of its lending in Russia from structural reform to poverty reduction. The European Investment Bank, unlike the EBRD where EU rates have predominant influence but not control, is the EU's own investment institution, which has over the years earned a rock solid reputation. It is perhaps not surprising that the EU did not wish to expose it to the risks of investing in Russia in the 1990s. But it should play a bigger part there as those risks decline. As the investment climate in Russia improves, the resources to be invested there by the European Investment Bank should also increase. The focus on investment in the private sector and on the framework for such investment remains, however, the EBRD's specific, and vital, contribution to Russian development.

By 2001, there appeared to be a reduction of chaos and corruption, a more liberal bias in government and an economy in better shape; and an experienced observer was able to write not only that Russian oligarchs were 'starting to build real businesses', but also that 'so long as reforms remain official policy, the case can be made that Russia is coming right'.[44] The EBRD itself had already formed the judgement that 'an increasing number of Russian corporations are taking a long-term view of business development.'[45] The Bank has played a part in bringing this about and is certainly well-placed to add momentum to the trend, using its leverage to help improve corporate governance and its influence for improving the institutional framework for investment. Its Directors from EU member states, who have predominant influence on the Board, should give the Bank any encouragement it may need to do so. Its initial capital of $12 billion in 1991 was doubled in 1997; and if its efforts are successful and it needs more, that should be provided.

Macro policies and financial aid

Shishkov recounts, in chapter two, Russia's encounter with western financial institutions in 1992. In January, the G7 governments were persuaded that Russia was launching serious reforms. They envisaged financial aid of up to $24 billion then 'dithered', as an authoritative voice has put it, passing the buck to the IMF, which provided only $1 billion of support to Russia's reserves. Russia was beset by hyperinflation and by the end of the year the reformers were out of power.[46]

Faster and fuller assistance might well have got reform off to a better start; and the decision to provide it could have been taken on the grounds that successful transition to a market economy was a matter of such political moment as to justify taking risks that were not within the competence of a financial institution such as the IMF. While the governments of European Community states could have their own judgements of that, the EC as such did not have the capacity to form a view. The experience of a very senior participant in its process of 'co-ordination' of monetary policy at that time was that in practice it 'never went very much beyond polite ritualistic consultation';[47] and this was not surprising in a matter where the instruments belonged to the member states, not the Community, and any decisions had to be taken unanimously. Less than three years earlier, France and Germany had, belatedly, pressed their G7 partners to agree to offer massive monetary support to what was then the Soviet Union, but Britain, Japan and the US had demurred.[48] The case for supporting the new Russian Federation was much stronger and there might well have been a substantial majority of Community member states in favour. But there was as yet no single currency which, given effective institutions for forming external monetary policy, would provide the basis for decisions in such matters. Meanwhile, it was only from the United States that effective political leadership in such matters could come.

The most influential source of external advice on the broad lines of Russia's policy for transition to a market economy was also American. Shishkov points out that Russian reformers themselves adopted the policy of 'price liberalisation and privatisation' first, regardless of other considerations, in order to ensure an irreversible break with the Soviet past. But it was also vigorously promoted by a group of advisers from the Harvard Institute for International Development. The cost was heavy. John Odling-Smee, Director of the department that deals with Russia at the IMF, observed that 'we underestimated the complexity of the whole transition process, in which the economic and political dimensions are intertwined. So, of course, did most observers. As a result, insufficient attention was paid, not least in Russia's own priorities, to the development of institutions and changes in governance that are needed to support institutions.'[49] It is not certain that advice from the European Union would have been more prescient. But it is certain that the policy led to private ownership without much development, together with the flight of perhaps $150 billion of capital in the 1990s. Given the range of policy orientations to be found in the Union, it is more than possible that advice from sources within the Union would have included other elements that could have helped to limit these depredations. But the Union lacked the policy-making credibility to ensure that such advice would have attracted Russian acceptance.

Given the shortcomings of its reforms, Russia was in no condition to weather the financial storm that broke in the Far East in 1998. Again, Shishkov recounts how, as Russia's financial situation became increasingly desperate, in July 1998 the IMF offered a credit line of $12.5 billion but actually advanced only $1 billion, while much vaster sums were being advanced to East Asian countries. This was understandable from the perspective of the IMF. But it did much damage, undermining international confidence in the Russian economy as well as support for the market economy among many of the Russian people though not, perhaps surprisingly and certainly crucially, among most of those who make or influence policy. Shishkov notes that Britain, France, Germany and some other West European states were more inclined than others to be helpful. But although the euro was before long to become the common monetary instrument of twelve of the member states, there was still no effective common policy in international monetary matters and no common position in policy-making in the IMF.

The euro is, however, the legal tender in those twelve states from 2002 onwards; and it has the capacity to put the Union on level terms with the United States, just as the common external tariff did in the 1960s in the field of trade. But the Union's institutions do not yet have the capacity to use it effectively as an instrument of external policy. The opt-outs of Britain, Denmark and Sweden are one weakness. But the institutional weakness is crucial and, although the Nice Treaty offers some improvement in the system for representing the Union in external monetary affairs, more will be required if the Union is to use its voting potential in the IMF, which far exceeds the weighted vote of the US, to pursue an effective policy there; and the same applies to its monetary relations with Russia, which should be a major element in the development of the EU-Russia partnership. Russia's principal statement of policy towards the Union has stressed the potential for use of the euro in the external activities of business firms and banks, in operations that would involve it in Russia's domestic financial markets, and in the Central Bank's exchange rate policy.[50] With an estimated up to $60 billion in dollar notes held by Russian citizens, moreover, they could have a substantial impact on the strength of the euro if, following the lead indicated by the government, they were to change a significant proportion into euros.[51]

The financial crisis of 1998 changed the climate of opinion about the 'Washington consensus' that had focused on liberalisation of trade and capital markets backed by macroeconomic stability, without attaching enough weight to strengthening the institutional framework in countries where it is not adequate to deal with the problems that may arise. In East Asia, the key weaknesses were the inadequacy of financial regulation and corporate governance. For Russia in particular, it remains necessary to emphasise the need for a sound institutional framework for the market economy as much as macroeconomic criteria like the control of inflation and budget deficits.[52] The Russian government has, in the past two years, made considerable progress in putting necessary reforms in place. But much still remains to be done.

It is a process to which Tacis and the EBRD make a valuable contribution, which is a vital element in building the Union's long-term partnership with Russia. Europeans, as Russia's close neighbours, have more than Americans to gain from a successful Russia and more to lose from Russian failure. They should provide the main input in the development of thinking beyond the Washington consensus and in ensuring that appropriate and sufficient resources are provided to put it into effect. Co-operation through the institutions of the PCA has been less productive than it might have been, partly because of the learning process required of each side for dealing with the other, but partly also because the Union has not yet given high enough priority to its Russia policy or been sufficiently effective in putting all the available instruments to work together for its success. This could bring great benefit not only to the relationship with Russia but also in the wider world, with other countries that face problems of transition to which the lessons learnt in a successful Russian experience could apply. This is just one example of the contribution that the partnership between the EU and Russia could make towards the building of a sound and stable world economic and political system.

Chapter 2:
The Socio-Economic
Situation in Russia

Yuri Shishkov

After ten years of efforts to accomplish reforms, and of the ordeals that the people of the country have had to endure, Russia has not yet been able to extricate itself from the crisis that is inevitable in transition from the command economy to a market economy. In 2000, its GDP was only 62.4 per cent of the 1991 level, industrial output 58 per cent, agricultural production 67 per cent and services 31 per cent. Income per head in 2000 did not exceed, on average, $2,740, which is less than one-eighth of the British level. True, official statistics do not record the shadow economy that is estimated at up to 40 per cent of Russia's GDP.

Transition to a market economy: economic conditions

Such a long and painful return by Russia to a normal market economy can be largely ascribed to the profound and long-term mutilation of the country's internal and external economic mechanisms and of the psychology of the people of Russia themselves by the 'builders of communism'. Since the 1880s Russia had begun to catch up with the Western industrial countries that were ahead of it in the level of production and the development of their market economy mechanism.[53] But this promising start was, unfortunately, broken off first by World War One and then by the 1917 Bolshevik coup that isolated

Russia for seven and a half decades from the world economic environment and set the country in opposition to it.

a) Soviet economic heritage

The Soviet leadership saw its historic task as fomenting in one way or another a 'world proletarian revolution'. After taking power, it was active in its support - both ideological and financial - for revolutionary outbreaks in Eastern Europe and Germany. When, by the mid-1920s, it had become evident that the hotbeds of revolutionary conflagration had been extinguished there, Moscow set its sights on preparations for a 'revolutionary war' with Western powers in the hope of arousing in this way the 'oppressed' masses to struggle against their 'oppressors'.[54]

This was expressed, economically, in an accelerated development of heavy industry as the material basis for rearmament of the Red Army. But the tackling of this task called for utmost effort in the country with its weak industrial basis, lack of domestic savings and no chance of obtaining foreign credits. Thus the so-called New Economic Policy (NEP), which was introduced by Lenin in 1921 and allowed some freedom of private enterprise, was superseded in the late 1920s by an explicitly anti-market administrative command and distribution system. This system was originally conceived as an instrument for squeezing resources from all parts of the economy and forcing them into the mass production of aircraft, tanks, artillery, other military hardware and ammunition.

Such a 'mobilisation economy' could only be of a toughly centralised type, excluding any elements of 'market spontaneity'. It is incompatible with either freedom to choose a supplier, or entrepreneurship, or market pricing. Prices, transport and other tariffs, as well as production costs in such an economy could, naturally, be only 'planned', that is, calculated by central government officials and obligatory for all economic agents. Clearly they did not reflect the real costs incurred by any given producers of goods and services, nor could they indicate the efficiency of economic ties of one or another kind. The senior managers of enterprises were moreover absolved of any responsibility for maintaining such efficiency because their products were supplied on instructions 'from above' to recipients who had been specified in advance, while these managers, in turn, received in a similar manner the raw materials, intermediate products, finished goods or services they needed from other enterprises.

An economy of this type can ensure high enough growth rates within a narrow range of industries for some time through stagnation or even degradation of the other sectors. But this was leading in the end to imbalance of the reproduction mechanism, a grave malaise of the entire economy, and a natural attenuation of its growth rates: precisely what happened in the USSR, beginning in the 1970s (see Figure 2.1).

But that is only part of the story. The lopsided development of the Soviet military-industrial complex over several decades brought about a deformed, two-humped sectoral structure of the economy. On the one hand, almost the entire scientific and technical potential of the country turned out to have been driven into the military-industrial complex and isolated there by a screen of secrecy from civilian industries. From this off-limits zone, only dual-purpose (civilian and military) technologies, and certainly not the most advanced achievements of the country's science and technology, leaked into other industries with great difficulty and to a limited extent. So for decades the civilian part of the Soviet economy languished in this routine, falling far behind the world level. On the other hand, the inflated metallurgical, fuel and energy complexes built way back during the early five-year plan periods, and needed for arms production and fuel supply for tanks, aircraft, naval ships and the like, were being favoured and constantly built up. All the other industries were sagging, as it were, in between these two 'humps' and were in all respects far behind the world level.

Agriculture had been subjected in the early 1930s to forced collectivisation in order to pump financial and manpower resources from the countryside into towns. It was consequently drained of vitality to the point where it could not provide enough food for a country that had previously been a major exporter of agricultural products. Beginning in the 1960s, the USSR started bulk purchasing of grain.

Figure 2.1: *Average annual growth rates of real GDP and GDP per head in the USSR, 1961-91 (in %)*

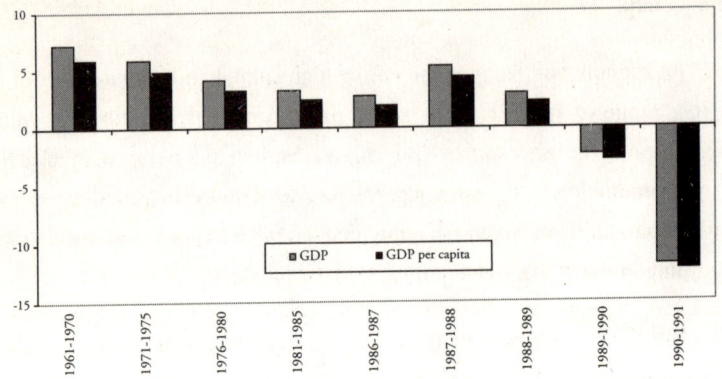

Source: *Handbook of International Trade and Development Statistics* 1993; ibid. 1995,
(New York: United Nations Publications), Table 6.2.

With its first-class scientists, inventors, designers and skilled workers concentrated in super-secret enterprises, labour productivity in the Soviet economy was by 1990 only some two-fifths of the British level, a third of the German and a quarter of the American.[55]

The mobilisation economy of the Soviet type was by nature resource-consuming and could develop for the most part extensively, that is by constantly making use of new material, human and financial resources. The vast scale of the USSR made it possible for a long time not to come up against the limits of these resources. But already in the 1960s, virgin lands, major oil and gas fields in easily accessible areas came close to depletion and for demographic reasons the inflow of new labour almost ceased. By that time it had become clear that agriculture could no longer be a reserve for financial resources for industrialisation. The Soviet economy reached deadlock.

An economic collapse was delayed only by a twelve-fold upswing in world prices for oil and other energy sources in the 1970s. The soaring prices helped to launch the exploitation of oil and gas deposits hard of access in north-west Siberia and drastically to increase their exports. From 1960 through 1988, exports of oil grew eight times, of petroleum products four times, of electric power 7.2 times and of natural gas 545 times.[56] As a result, the bias of the production structure towards basic industries became still more exaggerated. But the Soviet economy received, in return, over nearly a decade about 200 billion 'petrodollars'. By the mid-1980s, however, world prices for petroleum had dropped significantly, and its exports could no longer maintain the financial stability of the sick Soviet economy.

Nevertheless, the respite granted by the world energy crisis was not used to reform the country's economy. The Soviet leadership could not forgo the 'gains of socialism', nor could it undertake reforms: it was engrossed in the mounting arms race. But the depletion of former sources of budget revenue evoked an urgent search for new sources. In 1985, for the first time over the past several decades, a state budget deficit appeared, which grew rapidly to reach by the end of 1991 a staggering 31 per cent of GDP.[57]

The lack of financial resources had to be made up for, on the one hand by foreign loans and on the other by printing money. But more and more hard currency was needed to service the foreign debt. To pay off old-standing debts, new debts had to be incurred. Foreign debt began to grow like an avalanche: in 1985 it was $28.9 billion, by the end of 1989 $54.5 billion and by the end of 1991 $95.3 billion. Moreover, whereas in 1985 the USSR had no overdue debts, in 1989 it underpaid foreign lenders by $0.5 billion, in 1990 by $1 billion, and in 1991 by as much as $4.9 billion.[58] The gold reserves had to be spent for these purposes: in 1989-91, they shrank by more than 1,000 tons and by the beginning of 1992 only 290 tons remained. This was no longer enough to meet even the country's maturing obligations and most urgent needs.[59] The situation regarding hard-currency reserves was even worse. By the end of October 1991 they had been completely exhausted. All payments to foreign countries were suspended. The country approached the brink of bankruptcy.[60]

The economy began at the same time to be injected with uncovered money supply in the hope of thus maintaining economic growth. In 1988 money supply M2 (money in circulation and fixed-term deposits) rose by 14 per cent, in 1989 by 15 per cent, in 1990 by 18 per cent and in 1991 by as much as 77 per cent.[61] While lavishly handing out money to enterprises and increasing payments for work in cash, the government could not match these artificial incomes with an appropriate quantity of goods and services, whose shortage rapidly intensified, while inflation was accelerating with each passing year (see Table 2.1).

Inflation became in fact a new, albeit covert, tax on the population, allowing the government to use its cash deposits with state-owned banks to fill budget gaps. But inflationary financing was suppressing investment in fixed capital. In 1988, the increase in such investment was 7.6 per cent, in 1989 4.1 per cent, in 1990 0.1 per cent, and in 1991 there was a steep fall of 26.2 per cent.[62]

Table 2.1: Annual increase of wholesale and retail prices in the USSR in 1987-91 (in %)

	1987	1987	1987	1987	1987
Industrial wholesale prices	0.5	1.0	1.0	3.0	230
Retail commodity prices	1.0	1.0	1.9	5.3	210

Calculated on the basis of State Statistics Committee data.

Expecting a further rise in prices, commodity producers began to withhold their products, keeping them in store, while buyers began to purchase any kind of goods to stock. The counters that already had very little to offer quickly emptied, while long queues of people keen to buy at least something, a feature typical of the Soviet era, assumed unprecedented proportions. The situation was truly acute, as could be seen from the following news report published by *Izvestiya* in January 1990: 'According to current accounting, as of December last year, the system of state trade, consumers' co-operatives, various kinds of workers' supply departments, and other supply and sales agencies had meat and poultry for five days of trading, sausage for one day, fish (excluding herring) for 10 days and butter for 19 days'.[63]

The Soviet economy was rolling headlong towards a precipice. 'The totalitarian regime had brought the country into a trap from which it was possible to break free only at the cost of great sacrifices', Yevgeny Yasin, patriarch of Russian reform economists, wrote in 1992. 'It was exactly at the time when the crisis reached its most severe phase and when a firm resolve was required to take extremely tough measures that this regime collapsed. Responsibility for carrying out such measures fell to the democratic leadership.'[64]

b) Costs of shock therapy

In conditions of imminent famine, a real threat of hyperinflation and international bankruptcy, no chance remained for economic reforms to be undertaken gradually as was the case for example in Hungary, Yugoslavia, China or Vietnam. So reformers had to start, not with privatisation of state-owned enterprises and creation of a competitive environment but with **liberalising prices and opening the domestic market** to imported goods. Certainly, privatisation of enterprises, their release from government tutelage and getting them accustomed to competition are a most important task in the process of transition to a market economy. But its fulfilment calls for development of a legislative basis, affirmed in practice and adjusted with due regard for the interests of the various strata of society. For this a lot of time is necessary, but reformers were very short of time. What is also most important is that privatisation is impossible without free prices and a market-based assessment of the real value of a given entity to be privatised. To save the country from economic disaster, the process had to be started with liberalisation of prices and foreign trade.

On 2 January 1992, nearly 80 per cent of wholesale prices and 90 per cent of retail prices were freed from government control. Exceptions were made only for some socially essential consumer goods and services and capital goods and services (in particular, fuel and transport services) because a drastic rise in their cost could have paralysed the operation of enterprises. However, even these controlled prices rose three to five times. Earlier, in November 1991, all restrictions on imports were lifted and barriers to the export of finished goods were removed, though the export of fuel and raw materials was subject to strict restriction. In addition the exchange rate was liberalised in part, and in summer 1992 a single rouble rate was established.

These shock measures helped solve a number of urgent problems. First, they rapidly saturated the market with domestic and imported foods and other consumer goods, averted famine and drastically cut the surging demand. Secondly, they withdrew from citizens and enterprises an excess money supply that was creating the monetary overhang and threatening to cause a collapse of the country's financial system.[65] Thirdly, they drastically reduced subsidies to unprofitable enterprises, which had to sell their products at fixed prices that did not cover production costs; and this decreased the need to print money. Fourthly, the mechanism of free prices, combined with an inflow of imported goods and services, introduced elements of competition, including competition among state-owned enterprises. All of this compensated, in part, for a delay in large-scale privatisation.

Table 2.2: Consumer and producer prices in Russia in 1991-2000 (annual average, percentage change over previous year)

	1991	1992	1993	1994	1995	1996	1997	1998	1999	2000
Consumer prices	210	1528	875	309	197	22	11	84	37	20.2
Producer prices	230	3280	900	340	237	50	15	7	67	31.6

Calculated on the basis of State Statistics Committee data.

Given all these positive effects, the shock liberalisation of prices and foreign trade inevitably had a number of negative consequences. In terms of economics, it dealt several heavy blows to the real sector. An upswing in wholesale and retail prices surpassed by far reformers' expectations and significantly reduced effective demand both for investment and for consumer goods and services (see Table 2.2). It proved to be higher than in all other countries with transitional economies, except Yugoslavia and Bosnia. The contraction of domestic demand entailed a precipitous cutback in production in industry, agriculture and, especially, the services sector (see Figure 2.2). As a result, employment began to diminish, while unemployment started to rise, though to a less extent than might be expected.

In addition, high rates of inflation were depressing investment, especially in those periods when prices for investment goods were rising faster than long-term interest rates, that is when such rates become negative and bankers refuse to grant long-term loans. As for enterprises' own current capital used for investment purposes, inflation was rapidly melting it away. Consequently, during the first year of reforms, investment in fixed capital fell by 40 per cent, then continued to decline much faster than GDP. Both the amount and the share of investment in fixed capital dropped to a critically low level (see Figure 2.3). If we take the EU, for example, in the 1990s the share of such investment in GDP was, on average, 20.2 per cent, with 21.1 per cent in Spain, 23.5 per cent in Austria and 25.6 per cent in Portugal.[66] But that was in sound economies. Russia, on the contrary, has to renew the technical basis in a number of industries almost completely and introduce new and more effective technologies. So the country is in great need of investment.

Figure 2.2: Production in industry, agriculture and services, 1992-2000 (1991=100)

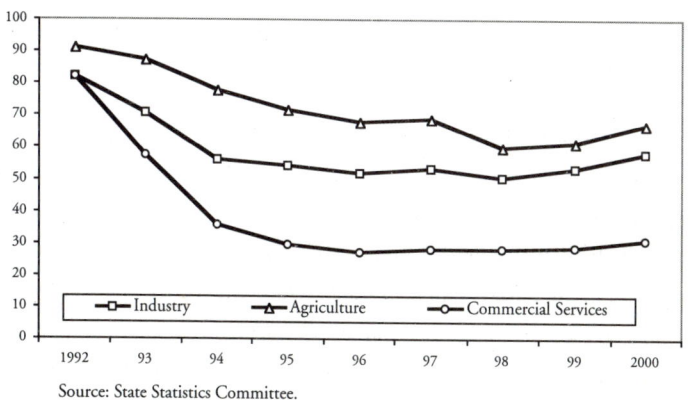

Source: State Statistics Committee.

Finally, the shrinkage of the domestic market compelled commodity producers to look for markets abroad. But the manufacturing industry inherited from the USSR was practically uncompetitive, apart from production of weapons and military equipment. Russia's fuel and metals are on the other hand by nature competitive, if their production costs do not exceed the world level; and such costs are generally low in Russia. Apart from this, domestic prices for most of them remained controlled and, at an early stage of reform, were one-half or one-third of world prices. Naturally enough, fuel, metals and other basic goods surged into foreign markets, in spite of export duties and other barriers imposed by the government. This aggravated yet more the deformation of the export structure towards basic goods. Whereas in 1990, oil and gas accounted for 14.7 per cent of Russia's total exports, in 2000 the figure rose to 53.5 per cent; and over these years the share of metals rose from 11.7 per cent to 17.9 per cent. The structure of Russian exports approximated to that of a developing country.

On **the social and political level**, the shock liberalisation of prices and the inflation that followed it engendered profound disappointment among the population and their negative attitude to reforms and reformers. Communists and other 'conservatives' were not slow to take advantage of this state of affairs, which enabled them to enlarge their representation in parliament significantly. In the 1995 elections, moreover, right-wing parties (reformers) did not obtain enough votes to be elected to the State Duma. This drastically deteriorated the political situation within the country and virtually halted the further progress of reform.

Though **mass privatisation of state-owned enterprises** was delayed for some time owing to a number of circumstances, it remained a second and most important component of shock therapy. In the Soviet Union, about 96 per cent of the country's total production of goods came from urban and rural state-owned enterprises and collective farms. The inefficiency of ownership and management of hundreds of thousands of enterprises by the state had long been evident. But for many reasons, first of all because the lion's share of enterprises worked for defence, this pattern of ownership was considered to be inviolable.

Figure 2.3: Index of new investment in fixed capital (right scale) and its percentage of GDP (left scale)

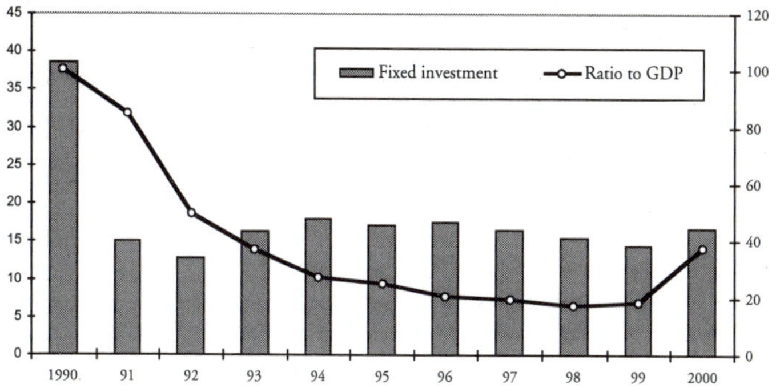

Source: State Statistics Committee.

Nevertheless, during Gorbachev's perestroika, timid steps started to be taken towards denationalisation. In 1986, production co-operatives were permitted in all sectors other than agriculture, opening the way for development of small-sized private business. In 1987, the 'Law on State-Owned Enterprise' was adopted, introducing financial and managerial autonomy of large and medium-sized enterprises: the so-called full cost-accounting. Subsequent laws and decrees expanded the range of enterprises with the right to deal on their own with foreign partners. By May 1989 about 5,000 state-owned enterprises had been granted the possibility to operate on foreign markets and 460 joint ventures had been established with the participation of foreign companies. Finally, in April 1989, the leasing of factories and equipment of state-owned enterprises by private companies was legalised.[67]

However, with the lack of a full-blooded legislative basis and the rapid erosion of government control, all these endeavours, especially the leasing of factories, made the directors of state-owned enterprises de facto full masters who were managing their 'property' at their own discretion. Denationalisation was acquiring a still more chaotic and ruinous character for the country. The wholesale plunder of the nation's resources started and dachas began to be built on a large scale for the party bosses and economic administration nomenklatura. This was not strengthening but, on the contrary, undermining the economy and discrediting the very idea of privatisation.

At the time when Russia began to carry on this process on its own (by early 1992), out of nearly 250,000 enterprises in the country only 70 were privately owned by individuals and 992 (non-agricultural) enterprises were corporately owned.[68] Two stages can be clearly distinguished in the history of privatisation in Russia: the first, from early 1992 to mid-1994, when mainly voucher privatisation was being put into effect, and the second, starting in mid-1994, when that made way for monetary privatisation.

Why was the first stage necessary? On the one hand, privatisation had to be carried out rapidly and resolutely in order to:

• introduce uniform rules for denationalisation of enterprises and put an end to the chaos of continued disorderly privatisation that represented, in substance, a peculiar form of pillage and was aptly dubbed *prikhvatizatsiya* (or grab-it-isation) by the people;

• bring the private sector as fast as could be to a critical mass that would render return to the Soviet past impossible. (After all, in Russia's parliament of that period the party of reaction was still strong enough, while the population's growing discontent with the first results of shock therapy was expanding the social basis of this opposition.)

On the other hand, in that initial period of reform there were no private owners of big capital who could invest it in state-owned enterprises. Nor could one count on foreign investors. But had there been such investors, no one would have sold them Russia's production assets cheaply. So an artificial demand had to be created within the country for the shares of the enterprises subject to large-scale privatisation. 'I and most of my colleagues, including A. Chubais, were sceptical about the idea of producing special instruments of payment that were to create a demand for property to be privatised, and were known as vouchers', wrote Yegor Gaidar. 'The risk of an inevitable and large-scale speculative redistribution of these instruments was all too evident. Of course, we wanted to get by without all these exotic devices and to use as much as possible the privatisation processes tried and tested in mature market economies. But a sober analysis compelled us to agree that to choose such a strategy in Russia would be to abandon the possibility of a radical reduction in state ownership. While gaining efficiency, we would miss the time when a breakthrough in restructuring the pattern of ownership was possible'.[69]

The quantitative effect was indeed impressive. Within two and a half years, 104,000 state-owned enterprises were turned into joint-stock companies or other non-state firms, though the state retained a share in the assets of some of them. Nine-tenths of all industrial workers became employed at private enterprises, half of them now working at the enterprises that had been privatised at voucher auctions. By mid-1994, there were nearly 40 million shareholders in Russia, more than in the USA or UK. Out of 148 million vouchers that were issued, 144 million were invested in production facilities or investment funds.[70] This undoubtedly changed the structure of ownership in Russia. By the end of 1994, the share of the public sector in GDP had dropped to 38 per cent, privatised enterprises (including corporations with state participation) accounted for 37 per cent and originally private enterprises for 25 per cent.[71]

As a result, there appeared in Russia a thin layer of private owners of capital, who had not yet become the middle class but who had taken steps in that direction. Besides, a system of institutional investors such as special funds, banks, etc. began to be formed. Finally, owing to the large-scale voucher privatisation, there appeared in Russia a corporate securities market without which any further advance towards privatisation is impossible.

All of this had great political significance. At an initial stage of reform, the alignment of reform and conservative forces in Russia remained quite unstable, and privatisation was needed, first and foremost, to tip the scale decisively in favour of the former. 'The voucher mechanism was not and could not be effective,' acknowledged Vladimir Mau, a close associate of Yegor Gaidar. 'However, it was the mechanism that ensured, in the short term, support for the authorities, while in the medium term it was helping to form a new class of owners with an interest in the stability of the new Russian economy. It was precisely this factor that made it possible to form an anti-Communist and anti-inflationary coalition and thus to accomplish the primary tasks of macroeconomic and political stabilisation.'[72]

From an economic point of view, however, this stage of privatisation turned out to be disappointing. As only a small proportion of enterprises (mainly in the light, food and furniture industries) were turned over to the local authorities for their obligatory sales at open and money auctions while most of them were being sold by means of voucher auctions, proceeds from privatisation were minimal or there were none at all. There was no increase in funds for modernisation of enterprises, and in most cases efforts to improve their specialisation also failed. In substance, everything boiled down mainly to redistribution of property rights.

At the same time, some models of voucher privatisation allowed workers' collectives to concentrate in their own hands 51 per cent of the shares of the enterprises where they worked. In many cases the directors of such enterprises managed to bring these stakes under their personal control and become in this way new business barons. The most pushful among them grew afterwards into oligarchs and began to exert influence on the government, parliament and even the president.

Figure 2.4: Balance of Russia's consolidated national budget (in % of GDP)

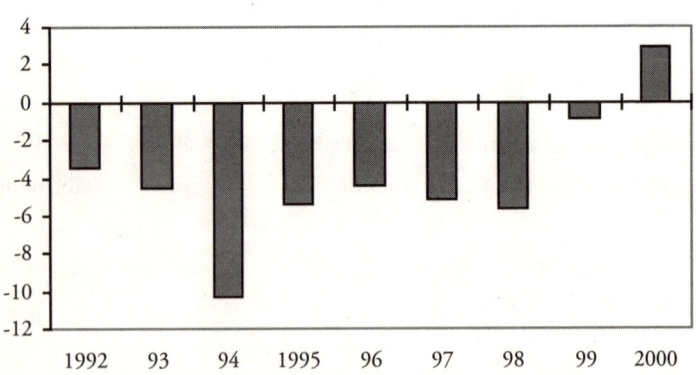

Source: *Die wirtschaftliche Lage Russlands*, Neunter Bericht, Teil I, Institut für Weltwirtschaft, Kiel, Dec.1996, p.10; *Voprosy Statistiki*, 2000, No.5, pp.58,64.

The second (monetary) stage of privatisation began in mid-1994 and was regarded by the government, first and foremost, as a source for supplementing the national budget which was by then enormously overstrained (see Figure 2.4). But there was almost no appetite for the shares of thousands of medium-sized and large enterprises that were unprofitable or bringing low profits. By that time, such vices as systematic non-payment by enterprises not only to state coffers but also to each other had become widespread. Burdened by accounts receivable and payable, enterprises were of no interest for investors. Likewise of little use were the new and non-standard methods of privatisation: loans-for-shares auctions, the transfer of federal shares to regional authorities to pay off federal debt to them, etc.

Figure 2.5: Number of privatised enterprises in Russia in 1992-2000 (thousands per year - left scale, cumulative - right scale)

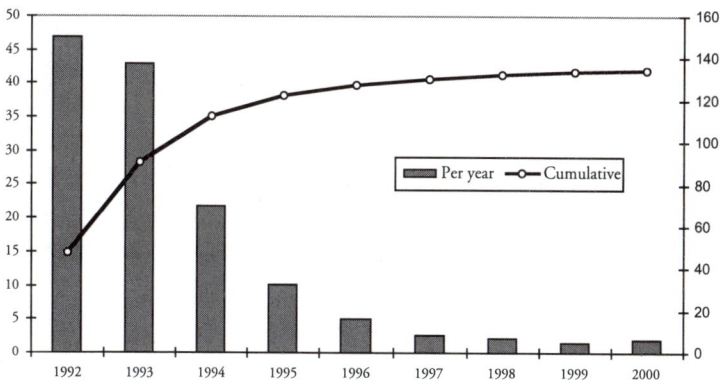

Source: Obzor Ekonomicheskoi Politiki v Rossii za 1999 god (Moscow: Economic Analysis Bureau, 2000), p.791; CIS Statistical Handbook for 2000 (Moscow, 2001), p.101.

All this led to a slowdown in the rate of privatisation (see Figure 2.5). Hopes of attracting additional resources to the budget were not fulfilled, nor did efficient owners emerge to reorganise production and adapt it to the requirements of a market. Outside owners conversant with the methods of up-to-date management and marketing did not appear as expected. This was partly due to the resistance put up by insiders (workers and directors) who had acquired controlling stakes back in the first stage, and partly because outsiders preferred to invest their capital in the financial sector where they could rapidly enrich themselves. If there were cases when they invested in production plants, they did it, as a rule, for the sole purpose of buying them (with the help of corrupt officials) at undervalued prices and, soon after, reselling them at a real and much higher market price.

As a result, after ten years of reform, relationships regarding ownership of industrial and other enterprises remain extremely intricate and controversial. The battle for redistribution of the ownership of privatised entities has not abated; and not only were there no efficient owners but, in general, they have not yet appeared. On top of that, regional and municipal authorities that have sought to acquire their share of advantage from this confusion have intensified their interference in the activities of privatised enterprises.

The financial collapse of 1998 and the breakdown of Russia's stock market froze privatisation for some time. By the end of 1999, about 295,000 state-owned enterprises and establishments were still federal and municipal property. But with economic recovery, conditions began to take shape for resuming this process. In September 2000, the government approved a new draft law on privatisation. It is intended to sell to private persons, within the next three years, more than 20,000 enterprises that do not bring, in practice, any resulting revenue to the state and, at the same time, resist any control at the federal or regional levels. This third wave of privatisation is expected to have as its aim not so much to supplement the budget as to restructure the economy. Now that the country's budget is in surplus, conditions are favourable for this. At the time of writing, however, the necessary legislation has not passed through all its readings.

An important component of transformation of the planned economy into a market one is **development of the credit and banking infrastructure**. This development was launched already in the years of perestroika and was of a largely spontaneous character. Before 1987, in the USSR there was a 'mono-banking' system where Gosbank (the State Bank) ensured redistribution of budgetary resources among industries and enterprises according to an approved plan. When state-owned enterprises were afforded some degree of economic independence and the establishment of co-operatives was allowed, the Soviet banking system assumed a three-tier structure. The State Bank remained at the top tier, responsible for emission policy, support of the rouble rate, ensuring interbank transactions and supervision of the activities of commercial banks. The second tier included five specialised banks: Sberbank (the Savings Bank), Vneshtorgbank (the Foreign Trade Bank), Promstroibank (the Bank for Construction and Industry), Agroprombank (the Agricultural Bank), and Zhilsotsbank (the Bank for the Social and Small Enterprise Sector). At the end of 1988 and in 1989, a large number of small private banks with an authorised capital of between 500,000 roubles and 300 million roubles each appeared in the form of co-operatives and joint-stock companies.[73] In 1991 Promstroibank, Agroprombank and Zhilsotsbank were transformed into joint-stock banks, independent of the government, with numerous territorial branches.

These branches and various co-operative and private banks formed the very fragile and vulnerable ground floor of the emerging banking system. The legislation of the new Russia encouraged the establishment of commercial banks and their number grew rapidly in the first years of reform. By early 1993, there were already 1,713 (with a total 3,135 branches), by early 1994 2019 (4,539 branches), by early 1995 2,517 (5,486 branches), and by early 1996 2,598 (5,586 branches).[74] However, taken as a whole, their assets were still quite limited. In the autumn of 1992, the World Bank noted: 'In fact Russia is underbanked. But it has too many small under-capitalised banks. Most of the new banks are owned by groups of enterprises, which get loans from their house bank - often at favourable interest rates. Many of these small banks exist only to borrow in the interbank market to finance the enterprises that own them. Consequently, the financial sector is not funding the most efficient enterprises, and the channelling of resources to loss-making ones increases the fragility of financial institutions.'[75]

Figure 2.6: Assets of Russia's banks, 1993-2000 ($ billion, left scale) and their share in GDP (in %, right scale)

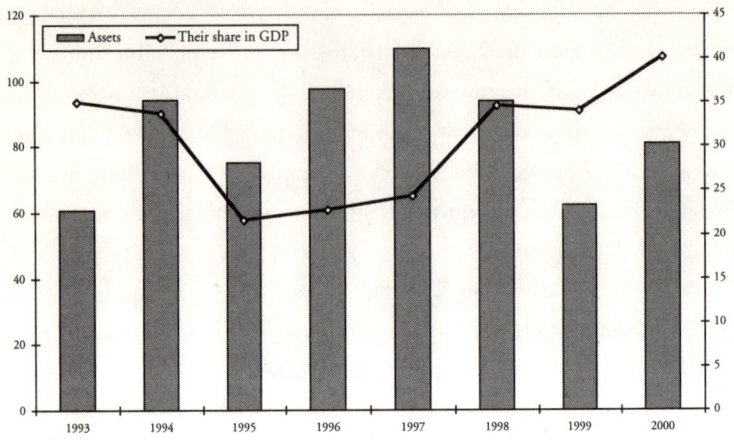

Source: Calculated from *International Financial Statistics*, IMF, various issues.

In this ocean of small and smallest banks, only about two score large and influential credit institutions towered above them. Although their assets were far smaller than those of the leading banks of Britain, France or Switzerland, they looked like pillars of stability and had the highest reliability ratings. Even though the Central Bank tried from 1997 onwards to improve the banking system, the situation remained practically unchanged. The number of small banks slightly decreased, but their assets continued to grow through interbank credit transactions and trading in government securities. The big banks also became keen on playing the securities markets and sought to attract foreign credits and the population's deposits at quite high interest rates without being much concerned about the balance between their assets and liabilities (see Figure 2.6).

Thus when the financial crisis struck, the ground began to shake beneath not only a great number of small and medium-sized credit institutions but also the majority of the most influential banks. A wave of bankruptcies swept over Russia. In 1998 alone, the number of commercial banks declined by 13 per cent while their aggregate capital fell by 40 per cent. According to expert estimates, the total damage caused by the crisis to the banking system was about 7 per cent of GDP, while the losses of bank clients (enterprises and the population) were 3-3.2 per cent of GDP.[76] Russia's banking system is only with difficulty recovering from that body blow. At the end of 2000 more than 1300 credit institutions remained, with only about a score of sufficiently strong banks among them. Nevertheless, in the context of steady growth of incomes in the real economy, banks' assets and profitability are gradually increasing (see Figure 2.7). The emergence of an effective banking system that merits the full confidence of depositors is, however, still a distant prospect.

Figure 2.7: Profitability of Russian banks (ratio of profit to capital)

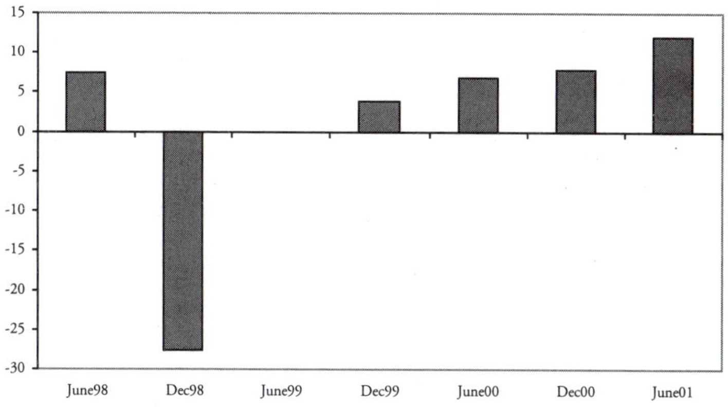

Source: Central Bank of Russia.

Agriculture remains the weakest point of market-economy reform in Russia. In Soviet times, the state was the monopoly landowner and allotted the land to state farms and collective farms, as well as to rural dwellers and some urban residents to keep their subsidiary holdings there. In 1990 there were 29,100 collective farms that made use of 171 million hectares of agricultural land, 23,500 state farms (359 million hectares), and 13,700 subsidiary holdings that had only 8.1 million hectares.[77]

The first private farms appeared in 1987-88 in the guise of agricultural co-operatives. First they were allotted land under lease and then they were granted life tenure of the land (but not ownership!), which they could bequeath as a legacy. A more or less adequate legislative basis for the further development of farms began to be created in Russia in 1990, as embodied in the Land Code that proclaimed private ownership of land (true, with substantial restrictions on the right to land tenure). Since then, more than 130 legislative and other acts have been adopted in this sphere. Private ownership of land was moreover confirmed in December 1993 by the Constitution of the Russian Federation. Up to the autumn of 2001, however, private ownership of land and accordingly a land market had not really been established. This has been due to strong opposition by left-wing factions in the State Duma and by numerous lobbies of collective-farm and state-farm nomenklatura that have striven to retain administrative levers that make millions of ordinary agricultural workers dependent on them.

At first the number of farms grew rapidly but then the growth slowed, to be followed, starting in 1996, by a decrease in the number of private farms (see Figure 2.8). Yuri Chernichenko, chairman of the Peasants' Party of Russia, wrote as follows to explain this process: 'Hundreds of thousands of the most enterprising people of the countryside and town were enthusiastic about the idea of unforced labour on their land, obtained plots of arable land, and spent years in creating an island of private life amid the ocean of post-collective-farm theft - and ruined themselves through their vain attempts to cope with taxes, price disparities, interest rates on loans, inflation and arbitrary officials.'[78] It should also be taken into account that in the USSR, unlike Central and Eastern Europe, the collective-farm system existed for six decades. Over the period, there were two to three generations of peasants who had no idea what it meant to have their own family farms and got accustomed to their status of farm servants completely dependent on the bosses of collective or state farms. Most of them are not prepared psychologically for independent farming and have a hostile attitude to those who made up their minds to take such a risky step. Finally, the heads of collective and state farms usually place every possible difficulty regarding the allotment of land and a share in assets in the way of those who decide to become farmers. So the process of establishing private farms has been extremely painful in Russia.

Figure 2.8: Number of farms (thousands, left scale) and the area of their land (mn hectares, right scale) at end of year, 1991-2000

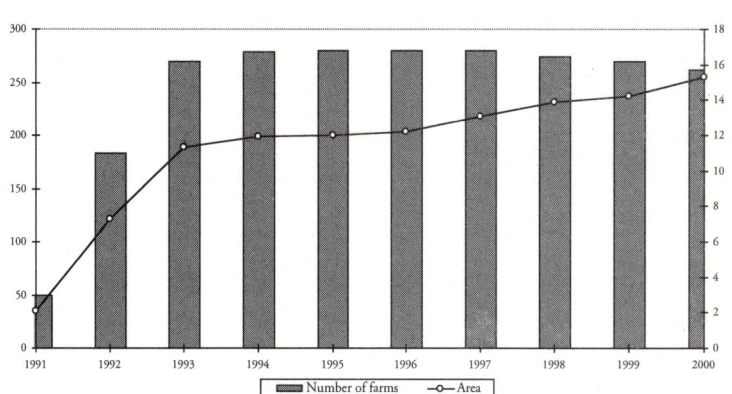

Source: M.P. Kozlov, 'Puti Dalneishego Razvitiya Fermerstva v Rossii', *Voprosy Statistiki*, 2001, No.5, pp.33-4.

Despite all these obstacles, however, 44 million Russian families have become owners or holders of plots of land.[79] The area of land belonging to farmers continues to increase through leasing or buy-out of land shares from those peasants who cannot or do not want to till the land on their own. By 1998, the private sector accounted for 11.4 per cent of the entire area of agricultural land, collective farms for 13.8 per cent, joint-stock companies and other new forms of farms owned by collective work-groups for 47.6 per cent, and 13 per cent remained state-owned.[80] President Putin has stepped up the process of land reform. In October 2001, a new version of the Land Code was adopted by the parliament, permitting market transactions for non-agricultural land. Procedures for purchase and sale of agricultural land are to be regulated by a special law.

Transition to a market economy: socio-political conditions

The Soviet economy's mobilisation model that was created in the pre-war period began already in the early 1950s to buckle under its own weight. The growing scope of production and diversification of industries led to the situation where the central planning agencies, Gosplan (State Planning

Committee) and Gossnab (State Committee for Material and Technical Supply), could no longer digest the huge flows of information from below and, all the more so, manage thousands of enterprises from above by former administrative command methods. A portion of managerial functions gradually shifted to the level of certain ministries and also, in some cases, to the level of large enterprises. In such a managerial cocktail, an ever bigger portion of decisions was made through iterative agreements between ministries and enterprises.

The development of this kind of 'centralised pluralism' gave rise to the shadow economy in its three main forms. At the level of *production*, in the form of illegal workshops that turned out products not accounted for officially and bringing big revenues to the 'workshoppers' themselves and the senior managers of the enterprises under whose umbrella they were operating. At the level of *sales*, there was an exuberant growth of 'shadow' trade whereby the goods produced by the 'workshoppers', or some quite legally produced consumer goods misappropriated through various machinations, were sold. At the level of *interaction between producers and wholesale consumers*, pushers of various kinds appeared rapidly in great numbers, who, for a certain payment, were taking upon themselves the functions of the State Planning Committee and looking for appropriate buyers for producers, and for suppliers needed by purchasers.

This underground economy grew steadily, giving rise to corruption at all levels and contributing to the accumulation of 'dirty' capital in the hands of 'teneviki' (those engaged in the shadow economy) and a huge array of officials. As such practices continued for almost four decades, they were firmly established in daily life and became a norm of conduct both for the senior managers of enterprises and for officials. But if the managers strive, under market conditions, to gain full independence, the officials have on the contrary a powerful interest in keeping private businesses dependent on government agencies (making it binding on private businesses to obtain various permissions, licences, etc.). Thus the process of removing the economy from state control has been deliberately impeded by an array of thousands upon thousands of officials of various ranks and levels. The adopted liberal laws get stuck in the labyrinth of the mechanism whereby the laws are supposed to be put into effect at both the federal and regional levels.

Another grave social and psychological legacy of the Soviet era is that most senior managers of enterprises are devoid of innovation experience. Why should they come up with ideas and improve the quality of products, if their buyer was known beforehand and was obliged to accept what would be supplied according to plan? The consumer goods market, in turn, was rigidly protected from competitive foreign goods and services by a solid barrier of 'state foreign trade monopoly': hence, not only the low quality of most Soviet investment and consumer goods and many types of services, but also the lack of executives who are able to think in market-economy terms. In the USSR there were several generations of managers who had no experience of competition or of penetrating sales markets.

Moreover, these managers became accustomed to the situation where, no matter how badly they worked, the government would provide them, without distinction, with financial and other assistance, and would keep their firms from going bankrupt. So when a new era of market economy arrived, they were concerned to acquire controlling stakes in their enterprises and change their chauffeur-driven Russian-made Volga cars for Mercedes, rather than to modernise production and bring the range of their products into line with the changing pattern of demand.

While losing precious time, they were sitting with their hands folded, waiting for the government once more to write off their debts or extend them interest-free credits. After all, under Soviet power the state was bound to save enterprises operating at a loss. At best, such senior managers, acting in the old way, were trying to lobby through 'their' deputies of the State Duma or 'their own' people in the government. Such behaviour in the most difficult period of reforms made no small contribution to the precipitous fall of production, the non-payment of wages and the growing discontent of broad strata of the population with the course of reform.

The Soviet model of economic management also had a pernicious effect on the psychology of ordinary citizens. Until the 1960s, collective farmers had no guaranteed payment for work. Only at the end of an agricultural year could they hope to receive an indeterminate share of the incomes in cash and kind that would be left over to their collective farm after all requisitions by the state and after setting aside reserves for the next agricultural season. Very often nothing remained after that and collective farmers generally received nothing at all. Industrial workers and the employees of state institutions were paid wages, according to a strict scale of wage rates, which were not to be above a certain ceiling. The scope for possible pay rises for more effective work was usually slim. So material incentives to work better and more were very limited: hence the indifference of the bulk of wage-workers and salaried employees to the results of their own work. No wonder that the minds of the masses were gradually gripped by the implicit stereotype: 'you pretend to pay me and I pretend to work.'

Modest pensions, other social security benefits, free health care and children's education were moreover guaranteed in the USSR. True, the level of such benefits and the general living standard remained low, but the benefits were paid regularly and without delay. Several generations became accustomed to this kind of paternalism. The eminent historian Richard Pipes wrote that the damage which can be caused by long-drawn-out dependence on charity from the state became clear after the disintegration of the Soviet Union, when a considerable part of the population, suddenly deprived of all-round state support and not prepared to support their life on their own, began to be nostalgic for the lost yoke of despotism.[81]

This was the psychology of Soviet society when it entered the era of reforms. The defence in depth by serried ranks of officials against removal of state control, the sentiments of ordinary citizens and most senior economic managers accustomed to dependence on support from the state, and indifference among broad masses to the market-economy opportunities that were afforded to them explain in large measure why in Russia, unlike Poland or Estonia, the attempt at rapid transition to a market economy did not succeed. The process assumed a protracted and painful character of which reactionary forces were able to take advantage, compelling Boris Yeltsin at the end of 1992 to dismiss the government of Yegor Gaidar. Instead of moving ahead along the path of reform, the newly appointed government headed by Viktor Chernomyrdin began to occupy itself, for the most part, in 'patching' financial gaps through a series of new loans obtained on the domestic and international credit markets. The economy continued to stagnate, non-payments among enterprises were growing, non-payment of wages to workers dependent on the state budget was rising, the living standard of the population was declining and the social basis for reforms was steadily dwindling. The political situation within the country became ever more destabilised, leading to a situation where Communists and other 'conservatives' were twice (in 1993 and 1996) on the point of returning to power.

Resolute and even extraordinary actions by Boris Yeltsin kept the country from moving backwards but could not prevent left-wing forces from strengthening their position in the State Duma. They were imposing on the country, year after year, a deliberately unfeasible budget, with expenses far exceeding revenues. Claiming to be advocates of the interests of the working people, pensioners and other low-income groups of the population, they pressed for increases in social expenditure, thus compelling the government either to resort to inflationary printing of money or to fall still deeper into debt. Neither measure allowed the government to fulfil the excessive budgetary obligations that it had taken upon itself, thus giving Communists grounds to constantly stigmatise the regime as 'anti-people' and to rock the boat. They were acting, in essence, according to the principle 'the worse the economic situation in Russia, the better', because in doing so they had more chance of returning to power.

The battle between reformers and restorers has also been going on all these years at the level of the entities of the Russian Federation: regions and national republics. In those regions where the Left has remained in power prices were, contrary to market-economy principles, quite often frozen for some socially vital goods and services, while their producers were being paid as in Soviet times through subsidies from the local budget. At first, such 'care' for people ensured the support of the electorate for 'red' governors. But such practices naturally led to excessive pressure on local budgets, their growing deficits, a reduction and termination of the subsidies to producers and, eventually, to their bankruptcy and to a curtailment of socially essential goods and services. For this reason in particular, the residents of the Far East's Primorye region have regularly been left without electric power and heating in winter, while the local governor (now, fortunately, a former governor) was just as regularly pinning the blame for these disgraceful things on the federal authorities.

This constant confrontation at all levels, between the past that has not yet gone for ever and the future that is not yet firmly established and is not always clear, makes it significantly harder for Russia to get out of the social and economic crisis that began before the disintegration of the USSR. Moreover, reform of Russia's economy was carried forward to a different extent in various entities of the federation, thus threatening the integrity of the Russian economic and legal space.

Attempts to reintegrate post-Soviet economic space are also a substantial burden on Russia's ailing economy. This task was declared right from the start to be a priority area of the new Russia's foreign policy. The aim is based in part on military-strategic considerations: sea ports, components of a single anti-missile defence system and other military facilities have remained in the territory of other CIS countries. The loss of these defence facilities in the Baltic countries was quite painful for Russia: hence Russian efforts to retain the closest possible ties with the other newly independent states. Economic integration with them was seen as a most reliable cement for keeping them in a single defence space. The priority for this aim has also been motivated by the great-power syndrome inherited from the USSR. As many policy-makers in Moscow see it, Russia cannot allow itself to lose its status of a great power and so cannot but have an extensive zone of influence. Finally, a certain role is also played by the endeavour to retain the CIS countries as guaranteed markets for Russia's manufacturing industry which is not competitive on the world market.

However, because of substantial differences in the levels of technical and economic development of the CIS countries, in the degree of removal of state control from their economies and a fundamental dissimilarity between the economic mechanisms operating there, all efforts to reintegrate them have naturally failed for more than nine years now. Trade and economic relations between the CIS countries have been maintained not on a multilateral but a bilateral basis. It should also be noted that because of the difference between world prices and the prices at which the CIS countries trade with each other, there is a covert subsidisation of some countries by others. According to estimates of the Centre for the Study of Foreign Economic Problems, of the Russian Academy of Sciences, the prices of Russian goods exported to the

CIS countries have in recent years been, on average, only two-thirds of the level of prices of these goods exported to 'far-abroad' countries (that is, outside the CIS), while the prices of goods imported from the CIS countries were one-third higher than the prices of such goods imported from 'far-abroad'. As a result, Russia has been suffering substantial losses, and should import and export tariffs be lifted completely in trade within the CIS, its annual losses could reach $7 billion.[82]

Even in relations with the more industrially developed Belarus, which is in a customs union with Russia, the lack of a real uniform customs tariff on the borders of Belarus with Ukraine, Poland and Lithuania has caused the Russian economy annual losses amounting, according to various estimates, to between $600 million and $6 billion.[83] Besides, some partner countries, aware of Moscow's interest in keeping the CIS in place, deem it possible not to pay for Russian supplies of energy resources and other goods. As of March 2000, the other CIS countries' 'energy' debt to Russia alone exceeded $4 billion, and if the credits extended to them by Russia are included, their total debt (including interest payments and penalty fees) was no less than $10 billion.[84]

Thus Russia has to pay a high price for the unsuccessful attempts to preserve the integrity of post-Soviet economic and defence space. The most modest estimates show that Russia is losing 3-4 per cent of its GNP annually as a result of its subsidisation, both overt and hidden, of the 'near-abroad'. That is almost as much as Russian expenditure on its defence or its health services, and about ten times greater than its budgetary expenditure on scientific research together with promotion of technological progress.

The 1998 financial crisis

The failure to complete reforms, and marking time by the government headed by Chernomyrdin, gave rise for more than five years to what President Yeltsin called, *post factum*, in his annual address to parliament in early 1999, 'a misshapen transitional system that has got stuck half-way from the planned economy to a market economy'.[85] One of the fundamental deformities of this system is that Russia's economy is split into two parts. The first part includes new or radically reconstructed enterprises that produce only what is in demand, make payments to each other only with 'real' money, and pay taxes and wages punctually. The other part represents enterprises that are leftovers from the Soviet era, which turn out obsolete products that are not in effective demand, make settlements with each other through barter, evade taxes and, as a rule, delay payment of wages. The watershed between these two parts lies not so much along the line of 'private versus state-owned' as along that of 'market-economy versus semi-market-economy' enterprises. The second group, unfortunately, still prevails and sets the tone.

Table 2.3: Russia's consolidated budget revenues and accumulated debt on taxes (billion roubles and %)

	1994	1995	1996	1997	1998	1999	2000
Budget revenue	164	410	534	654	625	1194	2218
including taxes	-	340	473	573	544	1003	1964
Accumulated debt	15	53	125	152	236	290	319
in % of budget revenues	9.2	12.8	23.4	27.8	37.7	24.3	14.4

Source: Obzor Ekonomicheskoi Politiki v Rossii za 1999 god (Moscow: Economic Analysis Bureau, 2000), pp.783, 786; Ekonomika Rossii za 2000 god (Moscow: IEPP, 2001), Section 1.3, p.2.

The big share of such semi-market-economy enterprises in the overall economic structure, combined with a poorly developed legislative basis, a weak tax service and rampant corruption, were the cause of increasing arrears of taxes to the federal and local budgets. In 1998 accumulated tax arrears to the consolidated national budget amounted to nearly 38 per cent of budget revenue (see Table 2.3). This was undermining the state's capacity to fulfil its budgetary obligations to the population and to institutions dependent on it.

From 1992 through 1998, wage arrears alone rose 11.4 times. The effective demand of both the population and enterprises was consequently shrinking. Whereas wage arrears in 1992 were 0.6 per cent of consumer spending, in 1995 they were 2 per cent, in 1996 5.9 per cent, in 1997 4.8 per cent and in 1998 5.8 per cent.[86] This impeded expansion of production for the domestic market, hindered attempts to get out of the crisis and, finally, made it impossible to enlarge the tax base: a vicious circle, indeed.

The government tried to escape from it by raising taxes on enterprises. But this undermined their financial position and prevented them from modernising and expanding production. So an ever-bigger number of entrepreneurs began to lurk in the 'shadows', concealing the true state of their affairs or not paying taxes at all. Chernomyrdin's government tried to find another way out of the budgetary crisis by vigorously printing money. But this led to accelerated inflation and a dangerous fall in the rouble exchange rate. There was also a third way to cover the budget deficit: resort to borrowing on credit markets.

At first the main source was loans from the Central Bank of Russia to the government. As can be seen from Table 2.4, in 1992 domestic loans were twice as high as federal budget revenues. Afterwards this ratio changed, but until 1995, domestic loans were comparable to budget revenues. Only starting in that year, the CBR stopped providing credits to the government, which began actively raising loans on the open market.

Table 2.4: Sources of borrowed funds for Russia's federal budget (% of GDP)

	1992	1993	1994	1995	1996	1997	1998	1999	2000
Budget revenues	14.6	13.0	11.9	12.4	12.5	13.1	10.9	11.8	16.0
Net drawings	43.3	15.1	9.9	4.7	6.8	6.5	4.8	2.0	0.6
Domestic	29.8	11.8	8.7	3.2	5.3	4.6	2.2	0.8	0.5
Foreign	13.5	3.3	1.3	1.5	1.5	1.9	2.6	1.1	0.1
Debt servicing	1.1	1.8	1.8	3.1	5.7	4.5	4.0	4.2	3.7
Domestic	n.a	0.6	1.3	2.1	4.7	3.6	2.4	1.7	1.5
Foreign	n.a	1.2	0.5	1.0	1.0	0.9	1.5	2.5	1.8

Source: Obzor Ekonomicheskoi Politiki v Rossii za 1998 god, pp. 150-51; Ekonomika Rossii za 2000 god, Section 1.3, p. 4.

For this purpose, beginning in the second half of 1993, it began to issue government short-term bonds (GKOs, also known as government treasury bills) and in addition, from mid-1996, medium-term securities - federal loan bonds (OFZs). The intention was that the government bonds would be a temporary instrument until the flow of tax revenues should increase.

This kind of borrowing has been used in many countries. But in Russia it had at least three very negative consequences. First, the development of the government securities market diverted the assets of enterprises and banks from the real economy. Instead of being invested in production of goods or services, capital began to flow into the GKOs/OFZs market where there was an opportunity to enrich oneself rapidly. It should be noted that at first GKOs had a very high yield: at the end of 1993 it was 170 per cent a year, at the end of 1994, 264 per cent and at the end of 1995, 104 per cent.[87] This made it possible for a short while to attract money to cover gaps in the budget but deprived industry, agriculture and consumer services of investment. As a result, the tax take declined and the need to issue GKOs/OFZs became still more acute.

Secondly, this did a disservice to Russia's banking system that had grown thanks to financial speculation yielding high profits, but was not able and did not want to be engaged in activities more useful for the country. By autumn 1992 the most widespread method of such speculation was to obtain in the West a short-term credit at an interest rate of 10 per cent a year, convert it into roubles and buy GKOs bearing interest of 30 per cent or more. The net profit was 10-12 per cent a year in foreign exchange.[88] To this end, many large Russian banks obtained enormous short-term credits abroad. By the beginning of 1998, the banks' foreign debt was estimated at more than $40 billion.[89] This meant that should there be a serious devaluation of the rouble, they would be insolvent in relation to foreign creditors.

Thirdly, and most importantly, the government engendered a self-generating process of uninterrupted issuance of government bonds. The government's domestic debt for them grew rapidly: in 1993 (at the year-end) it was $0.2 billion, in 1994 $4.6 billion, in 1995 $16.8 billion, in 1996 $46.8 billion and by mid-1998 it was $80 billion.[90] To pay off the debt for the previous issues, new loans had constantly to be raised. The amount of government bonds in circulation rose from 0.2 billion roubles at the end of 1993 to 274 billion roubles at the end of 1997 or, adjusting for inflation, to 28 billion roubles, that is, by 140 times! This financial pyramid was growing steadily, with an ever-bigger part of proceeds from the sales of GKOs/OFZs going towards paying off the debt for these bonds. By June 1998, the cost of interest and repayment of debt by far exceeded the proceeds from newly issued bonds.

A possible collapse of the pyramid of GKOs/OFZs was coming closer to reality. Foreign investors with much experience in such matters (their share in this market reached 32 per cent) began to pull out of the market at the end of 1997. To keep them in place, in January 1998 the government removed restrictions on non-residents' transactions, including restrictions on the repatriation of their profits. This enabled the non-residents, in case of a financial panic, to effect a massive repatriation of their capital from Russia, thus inevitably entailing a surge in the demand for dollars and a collapse of the rouble exchange rate.

These domestic problems were complicated by external factors, starting in autumn 1997. As early as May 1998, the financial crisis in Indonesia caused tensions on Russia's credit market and provoked an outflow of residents' and non-residents' funds. To keep them in place, the CBR trebled the refinancing rate - up to 150 per cent a year. This somewhat delayed an impending disaster. But it was inexorably approaching under the impact of another factor. The financial crisis of that time in South-East Asia caused a slowdown in economic growth rates in many countries and, consequently, a falling-off in demand for energy resources and an ensuing decline in world prices for liquid fuel. By August 1998, oil prices had fallen by 40 per cent from their level at the beginning of 1997. This was a heavy blow for Russia because one-fourth of its budget revenues came from oil producers and exporters. These losses could have been compensated at least in part by devaluation of the rouble and by increasing in this way the competitiveness of Russia's oil and other basic resources on the world market. But as has been said above, such a step would have led to a collapse of the national banking system. Russia found itself in a desperate financial situation.

The newly appointed government headed by Sergei Kiriyenko and approved by the Duma on 24 April 1998 cut budget expenditure by $6.7 billion and submitted to parliament a package of closely interrelated laws intended to save the financial system. However, the Duma was busy making preparations, at the initiative of the Communists, for impeachment of President

Yeltsin. The destiny of Russia's economy receded into the background. Apart from this, Communists could not forgo the pleasure of tripping up Premier Kiriyenko who had been thrust by the President upon the Duma under the threat of its dissolution. In mid-July, the Duma turned down a number of the most important draft laws submitted by the government, denying it a possibility to make use of even the small chance that still remained.

In this situation, as early as in July, a panic flight from the rouble to the dollar began and the price of Russian securities started to fall. Banks were no longer able to pay off debts and make tax payments, while the Finance Ministry, in turn, found itself by the beginning of August unable to ensure even current budgetary payments. The government and the CBR had no choice but to seek an optimal formula for acknowledging insolvency. And so, on 17 August, they announced three decisions: suspension of GKOs/OFZs debt servicing; widening the band within which the CBR had till then kept the rouble exchange rate; and a three-month moratorium on repayment of foreign debts to private banks. The Russian publicist Eduard Bernstein compared the decisions with moving Russia's ailing economy from an intensive care ward to an operating theatre. He wrote: 'The operation was conceived to be undertaken in two stages: within a week after these three incisions the intention was to come to terms with Western creditors on a concerted variant of rescheduling GKOs, and within a month and a half or two months, on a decision to satisfy all parties regarding commercial banks' debts. The logic of such operations was in line with the logic of intensive care: to convince the creditors of the borrower's reliability and respectability. But after the first stage of the operation the team of surgeons was discharged and the patient was moved not even to an intensive care ward but to an ordinary hospital ward.'[91] The President dismissed the Kiriyenko government.

Along with positive results that will be described below, default doomed Russia to severe troubles. The rouble exchange rate fell by three-quarters and the population's real money incomes during 1998-99 declined by 28 per cent, that is to the level of the most difficult year, 1992. The banking system, with the exception of a few large and medium-sized banks, collapsed, and many citizens lost their deposits. Some entities of the federation stopped transferring taxes to the federal budget and the country's unified budgetary space was jeopardised. Gross domestic product declined, as compared with 1997, by 4.9 per cent.[92] Russia lost for a long time the confidence of the international economic community and the inflow of foreign investment slowed down drastically.

External causes of the crisis

As has been shown above, the unsuccessful reform of Russia's economy and then the 1998 crisis were caused, above all, by the elements of socialism inherited from the Soviet era in the economy, the social sphere and the psychology of society. The incompetent macroeconomic policy pursued by the Chernomyrdin government and the confrontation between the President and the Duma made a big contribution to bringing this crisis to a head. But some part of the causes lies outside Russia.

From the very outset, the attitude of the West to the new Russia was ambiguous. On the one hand, both the USA and the West European countries welcomed the democratic changes that had been launched, the intention to create a market economy and the 'deideologising' of Moscow's foreign policy. But on the other hand, Russia was viewed as a big military power that inherited the nuclear potential of the entire Soviet Union and, at the same time, some great-power ambitions. It is probably for this reason that the West's assistance to Russia in carrying out its reforms was much more restrained and circumspect than the assistance provided to other post-Soviet countries.

True, at first the West promised lavish financial support. In January 1992, during a visit by Yeltsin and Gaidar to London and Washington, the British and American leaders were convinced of the genuine nature of the economic reforms that had been started and three months later the G7 announced $24 billion worth of large-scale aid to Russia. But things did not go beyond mere promises. For various internal reasons the G-7 countries did not start to allocate money from their own budgets and shifted the problem onto the IMF, though at that time Russia was not even a member of the organisation. It was several months before Russia could enter the IMF. Meanwhile, it was 'in the most critical period, from January to April 1992', Gaidar noted, 'that even a few hundred million dollars of spare foreign-exchange reserves would have seriously enlarged our freedom of economic manoeuvre.'[93] When at last, in July 1992, the IMF allocated $1 billion to supplement Russia's foreign-exchange reserves, the government's stabilisation programme had already begun to disintegrate.

It should also be noted that the IMF constantly attached the disbursement of each tranche to various conditions that, on the basis of world experience, seemed to be correct but often did not take into account the specific economic and political situation within Russia. In particular, the IMF frequently posed conditions that could not be approved by the conservative Duma, even though the IMF was fully aware of it.

Worthy of special note was the behaviour of the IMF on the eve of the August crisis and after it. In the summer of 1998, when the Kiriyenko government was making desperate attempts to prevent a financial collapse, the top management of the IMF took a wait-and-see stance and was in no hurry to reach out a helping hand. Moreover, when Anatolii Chubais, as special envoy of the President, came to hold negotiations on granting an urgent stabilisation credit to Russia, M. Camdessus, the IMF's Managing Director, was inaccessible.[94] In the meantime, special letters were received from thirteen western states, demanding that Russia repay in the nearest future $2 billion worth of long-standing Soviet debts, without waiting for their official maturity date in December 1998.[95] It was with great difficulty that the top management of the IMF was persuaded to open a new credit line worth SDR 8.5 billion (about $12.5 billion), of which Russia in fact received only SDR 675 ($890 million) in the second half of July 1998. In addition to that, $400 million was lent by Japan. As is generally known, in a similar crisis situation the IMF opened for Thailand a credit line of $17.2 billion, for South Korea $10 billion with a promise to increase it up to $60 billion, for Indonesia $18 billion with a promise to increase it up to $43 billion, and for Brazil $41.5 billion.[96] These comparisons hardly need comment.

Subsequently, obtaining each tranche was always preceded by an exhausting round of negotiations. Altogether, in 1998 Russia received from the IMF SDR 675 million and in 1999 SDR 471 million. (Since 2000, it has renounced the Fund's credits.) Overall, the loans obtained from the IMF from 1992 to 1999 totalled SDR 15,596 million.[97]

The conduct of the Western banking community is also a cause of regret. George Soros published a letter in *The Financial Times* on 14 August, observing that Russia was in a critical condition and international assistance was needed. Irrespective of his intentions, the letter provoked a massive flight of capital from Russia's securities market and drastically accelerated an impending crisis. When the crisis broke out, leading banks of the member countries of the Paris Club of creditors categorically demanded that the government of Russia alter the procedures for exchange of government bonds, threatening to seize the Russian banks' assets, Russia's real estate and other property abroad. Lawsuits began to be prepared and lobbying was started among the IMF, the World Bank and the G7 governments. The US Chamber of Commerce demanded that Russia introduce a tax code protecting the interests of foreign capital, allow production-sharing agreements to be instituted in the country, completely compensate for the losses of Western investors from the moratorium on the payment of GKOs/OFZs debts ($10-15 billion), make high-profit rate assets accessible to foreigners, etc.[98] In short, they seized the opportunity to try to bring Russia to its knees and force it into an economic surrender like the one they had managed to impose on a number of developing countries during the outbreak of the debt crisis in the early 1980s.

However, the reasonable stand taken by the leaders of Germany, France, Britain and some other West European countries made it possible, in the end, not only to settle the problem relating to the Moscow-declared moratorium but also to restructure Russia's total accumulated debt to the members of the Paris Club. This also served as an example for the London Club of creditors. With the first signs of economic recovery in Russia at the beginning of 2000, however, the leading members of the Paris Club once again adopted a tough stance in relation to Russia.

Chapter 3:
Russia's Policy towards the EU

Yuri Shishkov

For many decades, trade and economic relations between Russia (and the Soviet Union as a whole) and the European Community were constrained by the conditions of the Cold War and were therefore quite limited. From the outset, the Soviet leadership regarded the Community as an 'economic basis of Nato': another version of the anti-Soviet bloc called upon to impede a further strengthening of the role of the USSR in Europe and the world. With this in mind, Moscow strove to bind yet more firmly to itself, economically and politically, those Central and East European countries that in the aftermath of World War Two found themselves in its sphere of its influence, and to prevent their direct contact with the Community. At the Soviet Union's insistence, the member states of the Council for Mutual Economic Aid (CMEA, also known as Comecon) did not have the right to hold negotiations on their own with the European Commission. Such talks could be conducted only by the CMEA Secretariat: in other words, only under the control of Moscow.

Repeated proposals by the Community, starting in 1974, to some of the CMEA states to enter into negotiations therefore went unanswered. Only fourteen years later, on 25 June 1988, when the winds of 'perestroika' began to blow in the Soviet Union, was a framework agreement concluded between the CMEA and the Community in the form of a joint Declaration on mutual recognition, which gave the CMEA countries the opportunity to regulate their trade relations with the Community on a bilateral basis. After those with Hungary, Czechoslovakia and Poland, the 'Agreement on Trade and

Economic Co-operation' between the Soviet Union and the European Community was concluded on 18 December 1989.

Under this agreement most-favoured-nation treatment was guaranteed and the EC was to abolish all specific quantitative restrictions on Soviet exports with the exception of some especially sensitive goods (rolled steel, textiles, etc.). Rules were specified for trade protection measures to be applied in certain cases. As in 1990 the Russian Federation accounted for 77 per cent of all Soviet exports and 68.5 per cent of all Soviet imports, this agreement concerned, for the most part, trade between Russia and the EC. Though the Agreement established only the most general rules for these relations, leaving many other problems unresolved, it created favourable conditions for the development of reciprocal trade (see Figure 3.1). One of the most important problems that remained unresolved was the status of Russia as a state-trading country, so that it did not qualify to benefit from a number of trade rules generally accepted among market-economy countries.

After Russia became an independent state and from the end of 1991 launched its reforms, liberalising prices together with domestic and foreign trade, preparations for a new agreement, taking these cardinal changes into account, were on the agenda. Besides, in that period during the Uruguay round of Gatt negotiations a new and more liberal concept of international trade was being shaped, which could not but have an effect on economic relations between Russia and the Community. So after long and arduous negotiations, on 24 June 1994 they signed a multi-faceted Partnership and Co-operation Agreement (PCA).

As projected under the PCA, relations between Russia and the EU (into which the Community had by then, following the Maastricht Treaty, been incorporated) were to become similar to those that exist between the EU and market economies. In the PCA the parties proceeded from the premise that Russia was no longer a state-trading country. Discriminatory restrictions that were in force during the Cold War period in relation to such countries were therefore no longer valid. According to some estimates, there had been up to 600 such restrictions, costing Russia several hundred million dollars a year.[99] Under the PCA, most-favoured-nation treatment for Russia was confirmed. In addition, the European Union extended the System of General Preferences to Russia as a country with an economy in transition.

Figure 3.1: Dynamics of Russia's foreign trade turnover with the EU-15 (in $ billion)

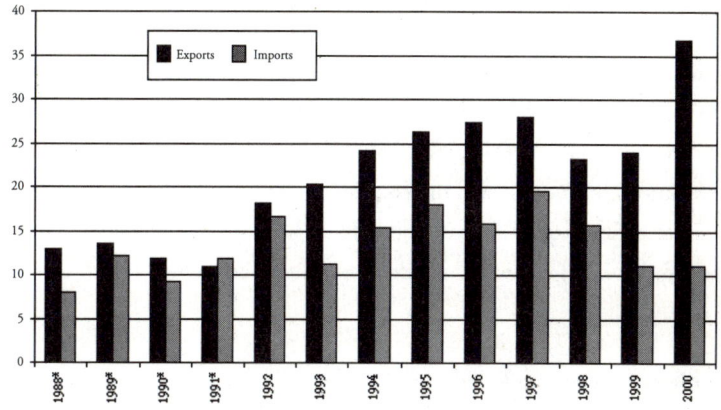

Estimates by the author based on the Handbook of International Trade and Development Statistics, Table A.1.

Source: Tamozhennaya Statistika Rossii.

The PCA put an end to the unilateral imposition of anti-dumping procedures without preliminary consultations. Quantitative quotas on the import of Russian goods to the EU, with the exception of textiles, steel and nuclear materials (trade in these three groups of products being regulated by a separate agreement) were abolished. Apart from trade, the PCA provides for more than thirty other areas of co-operation between the EU and Russia, including industrial, scientific and technical co-operation, co-operation in the fields of the power industry, extractive industries, agriculture, transport, space exploration, environmental protection, education, personnel training, etc. As Russia cannot, because of its size, become a full member of the EU, such a partnership can be considered an optimal form of co-operation between the parties.

As the ratification of the PCA by all the fifteen EU member states and assent by the European Parliament took a long time, an 'Interim Agreement between Russia and the EU on Trade and Trade-Related Matters' was signed on 17 June 1995 and came into effect on 1 February 1996. The agreement included many of the PCA's provisions, and stipulated for Russia more favourable conditions of trade than those that exist in its relations with, for example, the USA and Japan. As we saw in chapter one, the ratification of the PCA itself dragged on for more than three years because of the first anti-terrorist operation in Chechnya and entered into force only on 1 December 1997. Since then, economic relations between Russia and the EU have been regulated by the PCA's rules, which are favourable to further development of the relations but do not exclude contradictions that arise in cases when the interests of the parties do not coincide. Three spheres of these relations, trade, finance and technical assistance, are discussed below.

Problems concerning trade

Russia and the EU are of economic interest to each other, first and foremost, as trade partners. True, this interest is asymmetric: whereas the share of Russia in the EU's foreign trade does not exceed 3-4 per cent, their share in Russia's foreign trade is 33-37 per cent. But for some groups of products, the picture is different. In 1996, for example, the share of Russia in the European Union's total import of oil products was 27.4 per cent, of non-ferrous metals 18.9 per cent, of organic chemicals 16.1 per cent, of timber 11.1 per cent and of ferrous metals 9.5 per cent.[100] In turn, Russia imports from the EU a large quantity of machinery and equipment (in 1997 the EU's share of Russian imports was 42.5 per cent), as well as of consumer goods that are either not produced within the country at all or whose quality does not at present satisfy Russian consumers. Thus both parties have an interest in maintaining and expanding reciprocal trade. But other and no less objective economic interests of the parties stand in the way of such expansion.

As regards Russia, its survival as an industrially developed country and its very future depend directly on whether it will be able to revive, modify and expand its manufacturing potential. As we saw in chapter two, it inherited from the Soviet Union a deformed structure of industry with inflated fuel and metallurgical complexes, a high technology defence complex for which the need had drastically declined, and with all other sectors of manufacturing under-developed. In essence, the question is: either Russia will be able within the next few years to breathe new life into the civilian sectors of this branch of industry inter alia by conversion of defence production facilities and by attracting direct foreign investment, or it will slide into the position of a fuel and raw material appendage of the West, notwithstanding its status of a great nuclear power. It is clear that in such conditions Russia has to ensure a reliable **tariff and other protection of those sectors of its economy that are in a critical condition.** This is its legitimate right and duty.

However, after many decades of state monopoly of foreign trade, when top priority was given to administrative measures to protect the domestic market, it is very difficult to establish a civilised system of protection. At the very outset, from the end of 1991 to the middle of 1992, in conditions of enormous deferred demand and a most acute shortage of consumer and investment goods, their import was not subject to either tariff or quantitative restrictions. Even value-added tax was not levied on imported goods. Moreover, at the beginning of 1992, the government was granting subsidies to importers so that vital goods from abroad could be sold within the country at controllable low prices. This measure, aimed at protection of low-income groups, was too expensive for the government, costing about 25 per cent of GDP at the beginning of the year and 12.6 per cent of GDP for 1992 as a whole.[101] So import subsidies declined steadily and were abolished by the end of 1993.

When the most difficult, shock phase of price and trade liberalisation was over, differentiated import tariffs were introduced in mid-1992, with a weighted average for manufactured goods of 10.9 per cent. Afterwards, tariff policy was determined not only by the need to protect domestic producers but also by two other factors: fiscal considerations and the endeavour to induce foreign partners to turn from the export of goods and services to Russia to investment in Russia's enterprises. It was largely for fiscal motives that, starting in February 1993, VAT and excise duties began to be levied on imported goods. Even though these measures led to a reduction of imports by 27 per cent, beginning in mid-1994 import duties were made still tougher. Nevertheless, they remained at half or one-third of the level of weighted average tariffs for manufactured goods in China (46.5 per cent in 1992), Thailand (42.4 per cent in 1989), Brazil (32.3 per cent in 1991) or Indonesia (25.4 per cent in 1993).[102]

With the adoption of the law 'On State Regulation of Foreign Trade' in 1995, the process of import liberalisation became more logical, streamlined and consistent. The rates of import duties were becoming ever more differentiated and the tariff protection of the domestic market tougher. But these tougher measures were unfortunately very often fiscally motivated. By the beginning of 1997, the weighted average rate of Russia's import tariff was 14.5 per cent, and if VAT is added, the prices even of goods that were not dutiable rose by 26-37 per cent when crossing the border. In 1995, aggregate customs duties made up one-fourth of all Russian budget revenues.[103] This substantially limited imports and, consequently, revenue from import duties, while driving many importers to lurk in the 'shadows', that is, pushing up contraband trade.

Nevertheless, Russia's import policy has been gradually taking a civilised shape. Since 1996, the rates of customs duties have been worked out in greater detail. The import tariff was increasingly based on the principle that the higher the degree of processing of a given product, the higher the tariff applied to it. As in most other countries, minimum rates have been set for imported raw materials, average rates for semi-finished products and high rates for manufactured goods. Such a pattern of import tariffs has been devised in order to improve the price competitiveness of manufacturing sectors that consume imported raw materials and semi-finished products and, at the same time, to protect from lethal competition on the part of foreign companies those sectors that are in a state of deep crisis but are capable of meeting a substantial part of domestic demand: automobiles, farm machinery, the light and food industries, and some other sectors of manufacturing.

On 1 January 2001, a new tariff schedule was introduced, under which maximum (30 per cent) rates have been removed almost completely, the number of products with rates of 25 per cent has been substantially reduced, and import tariffs have been unified among groups of homogeneous consumer goods. As a result, the weighted average of Russian import tariffs dropped to 10.7 per cent. In February 2001, it was decided to make a still bigger reduction of tariffs on the import of nearly 1,000 types of machinery and equipment that either have no Russian equivalents or help to upgrade the technical level of the domestic industry.

As for non-tariff measures of protection, from the outset they excluded import quotas. Only a limited range of products that can threaten human life or public order are subject to licensing, including chemicals for plant protection, medicines, industrial waste, armaments, ammunition, nuclear materials and technologies, dual-purpose products, drugs, psychotropic substances and poisons, as well as precious gems and metals. As fake alcoholic drinks were flooding into Russia, causing a great many cases of poisoning and even many deaths, ethyl alcohol and vodka were included in 1997 in the list of goods subject to licensing. In addition, because of numerous machinations involved in evading duty and tax payments when importing goods under a scheme for processing of Russia's raw materials abroad and bringing finished products back to the country, the licensing of such transactions was introduced.

Improvement of the structure of Russia's industry implies not only protection of certain sectors of the domestic market but also **regulation of the export of domestically produced goods and services**. Because of the specific features of the industry's sectoral structure inherited from the USSR, in the early period of reforms this regulation was aimed not so much at encouraging export of manufactured goods as at restraining export of a number of basic resources. As has been said above, after the liberalisation of foreign trade a big difference between domestic and world prices (see Table 3.1) induced a large-scale export of Russian energy resources, non-ferrous metals, cellulose, etc. This was damaging Russia in three ways.

First, resources began to be exported in great quantity by completely unqualified people, very often below the world price. In this way, they were depressing prices on the world market and making conditions worse for trade in that sector, while Russia was losing part of its due export earnings. Secondly, such a massive 'throwing away' of resources was giving Western countries grounds to initiate anti-dumping proceedings which closed their markets for all Russian exporters of the given product group for a long time. Thirdly, uncontrolled export of some types of fuel often caused shortage on the domestic market and an inevitable upswing in domestic prices, thus destabilising the economic and political situation within the country.

Table 3.1: Relationship between domestic and world prices for Russia's commodities (world prices = 100)

	1993	1994	1995	1996	1997	1998	1999
Natural Gas	60	64	58	57	56	57	57
Oil	40	48	64	62	64	63	35
Electrical power	18	21	23	21	25	24	24
Steel	29	35	65	61	73	43	28
Aluminium	37	34	42	50	44	49	43
Nitrogen fertilisers	44	39	38	43	44	35	35
Cellulose	34	45	26	44	38	33	38
Timber	16	16	18	20	19	14	7

Calculated on the basis of *Rossiya Na Puti v VTO: Otraslevoi Razrez* (Moscow: IMEMO - Institute of World Economy and International Relations, 2001), pp.95-99.

A major specific feature of Russia's export policy is therefore to restrict the export of a number of basic goods. In 1991-92, administrative methods inherited from the past were used almost exclusively for this purpose. They included export quotas and licences, together with obligatory registration of the exporters of strategically important raw materials. In 1992-93, 75 per cent to 80 per cent of all Russian exports were subject to licensing. The obligatory sale by exporters of 40 per cent of their foreign-exchange earnings, starting in January 1992, became another important instrument for restraining exports. Finally, to guarantee a high professional level of exporters and return of their foreign-exchange earnings to the country, during the first years of reforms a category of 'spetseksportery' (special exporters) was established for these purposes: only organisations specially selected by the Ministry of Foreign Trade had a right to export oil and petroleum products, natural gas, electric power, non-ferrous metals, nitrogen and phosphate fertilisers, cellulose, coniferous industrial timber and wheat. These measures helped prevent an upswing in domestic prices for energy resources and industrial raw materials, which could have paralysed Russian manufacturing industry.

Starting in mid-1992, however, administrative measures began to be supplanted by economic regulatory instruments in the form of export tariffs. The list of goods and services subject to quotas and licensing was gradually reduced and, starting in mid-1994, quotas were abolished, though licensing remained in force for a narrow range of products whose export is regulated by Russia's international obligations and for those products under special export regimes (including armaments and dual-purpose goods, medicines, nuclear materials, etc.). In 1995, moreover, the status of special exporters was abolished. The level of export duties was meanwhile gradually being reduced and on 1 April 1996 they were abolished. The only exception was oil export tariffs which, since March 2000, have been in force automatically: with world oil prices below $12.5 a barrel, export is not subject to duty at all; with oil prices between $12.5 and $15 a barrel, the duty is $2 a ton, with prices at $15-17.5 a barrel, it is $5 a ton, and so on. If world prices rise above $32.5 a barrel, Russian exporters will have to pay the government $48 a ton.[104]

Since 1993 measures have also been applied for the promotion of Russia's manufactured goods in foreign markets. The law 'On Customs Tariff' provided for a number of such measures: direct credits for export transactions, government guarantees for commercial banks' credits and export credit insurance. All of this was to help improve the structure of Russian exports. However, because of the continuing budget deficit, there was never enough money for these purposes.

Another aspect of Russian foreign trade policy is aimed at **overcoming external barriers to Russia's exports**. The main obstacle is that Western partners still do not recognise Russia as a country with a market economy, with consequent very tough anti-dumping practices. It should be recalled that in 1978-88, the European Commission brought 40 charges against Soviet exporters, accusing them of dumping, most of which led to the imposition of additional import duties.[105] As domestic prices in the USSR were determined not by the market but by the government, during such anti-dumping proceedings the Commission was guided not by Russia's real domestic prices for a given commodity but by prices for a similar commodity in a 'substitute' country. (For instance, during proceedings on dumping of Russian aluminium, Canadian aluminium was chosen as an analogue, disregarding a big difference in the cost of electric power in Russia and Canada.) Naturally enough, such methods of calculation distorted the real picture and resulted in the imposition of unjust penalties; and the victims were not only the suppliers in question but also an entire branch of industry on the grounds that it was not a market-economy one.

The same practices persisted after the disintegration of the USSR. At the beginning of 2001, the total number of this kind of restrictive measure in relation to Russian exporters exceeded a hundred, including sixteen actions brought by the EU, twelve by the USA, nine by India, etc.[106] True, unlike the USA that until now does not recognise Russia's economy to be a market economy, the EU has since 1 July 1998 granted Russia the status of a country with a market economy in case of anti-dumping proceedings. But even here, the status has not been recognised unconditionally: in each case it has to be proved that a given enterprise operates as a market-economy one. So Russia has been striving persistently for its full recognition as a country with a market economy.

There have also been not a few conflicts between Russia and the EU over rules for trade in textiles and steel. To protect its textile industry, already in the early 1980s the EU imposed import quotas on 35 categories of competitive products from the USSR. The reason was the invasion of Soviet troops in Afghanistan. But even after they were pulled out of that country, the same trade regime remained in force. By the mid-1990s, Russia did not have a right to export more than ecu 140 million of textiles a year (the ecu being the precursor of the euro). At the same time, exporters from the EU member countries were supplying ecu 580 million of such products to Russia a year.[107] Moscow repeatedly suggested the abolition of quotas on both sides but without success. Only after the production of carpets in Russia had declined to one-seventh of the level of 1993, and the Russian government established in December 1997 a temporary quota of $100 million (for a year) on the import of carpets and carpet coverings from the EU, did progress in negotiations begin to be manifested; and since 1998, all quantitative restrictions in reciprocal trade in textiles and clothing have been abolished. The parties undertook not to establish them in future too, apart from exceptional cases.

A certain ground for contradictions also exists in trade in steel because both parties are major producers. Its quality everywhere is approximately the same and the price depends on production and transport costs. As these costs remain lower in Russia than in Western Europe, Russian steel is highly competitive on the EU market; and until 1996 the supplies of Russian steel to the EU countries were limited by annual quotas that were established unilaterally. Later on, these supplies began to be limited by special agreements between Russia and the EU.

Two such agreements have been in force for the period 1997-2001. They include limits set to the supplies of certain types of sheet and rolled steel, which are in the European Coal and Steel Community's list of products, and 'double control' (without quantitative restrictions) over other types of rolled steel, which are not within the list. These agreements made it possible to exempt nearly nine-tenths of Russia's steel exports to the EU from restrictions. Russia has become a major supplier of this product: by 2000 its share in total EU imports of steel reached 16 per cent, with its share in the import of semi-finished products standing at 45 per cent and in the import of sheet products, rolled steel and pipes at 10 per cent.[108] The EU has moreover been ready to open its market fully to Russian steel by the end of 2001, if Russia can establish legislation for providing government subsidies and for environmental protection in this branch of industry that meet the standards of the European Union. This is very difficult to do in present-day conditions in Russia.

A special field of Russia's external trade relations is **trade in commercial services**. This is a relatively new problem for the country that for decades was practically isolated from the rest of the world. Statistics of Russia's foreign trade in services are available only from 1994 (see Table 3.2). As regards the scope of services exports, before the 1998 crisis Russia surpassed such countries as India, Brazil and Indonesia, and as regards imports, Australia, Sweden,

Brazil and Mexico. Tourism accounts for half of Russian trade in services. The number of visits by Russian tourists abroad far exceeds that of foreign tourists to Russia, giving rise to a deficit in services trade as a whole. Transport services are the next most important. Russia is most competitive in the communication services sector (thanks to its space communication facilities) and in the sphere of scientific and technological R & D (trade in licences and royalties). At the same time, it is significantly behind its foreign partners for trade in construction and financial services. Among Russian exports there are almost no marketing, managerial, auditing and other relatively new types of services.

Table 3.2: Russia's foreign trade in services ($ billion)

	1994	1995	1996	1997	1998	1999
Exports						
World	8,425	10.568	13,283	14,079	12,373	9,087
EU 15	n.a	4,030	4,218	3,915	4,223	2,968
Share of EU (%)	n.a	38.1	31.8	31.8	34.1	32,7
Imports						
World	15,140	19,971	18,405	18,836	16,219	12,427
EU 15	n.a	4,097	4,644	4,571	4,188	2,930
Share of EU (%)	n.a	20.5	25.2	24.3	25.8	23.6

Source: International Trade Statistics 2000, Eurostat, pp.173, 176.

The EU countries are Russia's chief partners in services trade: they account for more than one-third of Russia's exports and nearly one-fifth of its imports. As in commodity trade, the interdependence is deeply asymmetric: the share of Russia in the EU countries' exports of services in 1998 was only 1.7 per cent and in their imports, 1.6 per cent. Nevertheless, Germany, France and some other EU countries are very interested in deepening and expanding an exchange of services with Russia, especially those that provide for a stable supply of Russian gas (construction of new pipelines), the launching of their satellites from Russia's cosmodromes, etc.

Like any latecomer to this area, Russia has to protect its services sector and create favourable conditions for bringing it up to the world level. However, the establishment of legal regulations in this area of foreign trade began only a few years ago, and much still has to be done to bring Russian legislation into line with world standards and the rules of GATS (General Agreement on Trade in Services).

Enhancement of interaction between Russia and the EU, and the process of adjusting Russia to fit in with the European economic space, largely depend on when and under what conditions Russia will join the WTO. The Russian leadership set its sights on accession a long time ago. Already in June 1993, President Boris Yeltsin officially handed over to the Secretary-General of Gatt a notification of Russia's intention to become a full member. It is expected that entry into the WTO will help create better, non-discriminatory and predictable conditions for the access of Russian goods and services to foreign markets, contribute to improving the structure of Russian exports, ensure adequate protection of its producers in conditions of a reasonably open economy and, at the same time, give Russia access to WTO mechanisms in settlement of trade disputes with partner states. But the way towards joining the WTO turned out to be much thornier and longer than had at first appeared.

In 1998 Russia set out initial tariff proposals on trade in goods and in 1999 on trade in services. Since April 2000, bilateral consultations have been started with WTO member states concerned, on issues where there is a direct conflict of economic interests between Russia and its chief partners. Now there are such negotiations with about 60 WTO members, and with 26 of them on access to the services market in particular.

Major difficulties arose, however. Demands have been posed that Russia bring down, within seven years, the average level of its import tariffs from 11-12 per cent to between 7 per cent and 8 per cent. According to estimates of Russian experts, this would lead to an increase in the country's total imports by almost 15 per cent, with an increase in imports of foodstuffs reaching 20 per cent and of light industry products as much as 25 per cent, leading to a decline in production in these two branches of industry by 7.2-7.4 per cent, and in Russia's economy as a whole by 1-1.5 per cent.[109] Apart from the food and light industries, protection would be needed for Russia's production of aircraft, automobiles, medicines and light chemical products. Among services, banking, insurance, telecommunications and some kinds of transport have particular need of protection.

Western partners also have serious demands regarding the level of Russian government support for domestic production and subsidies for exports of agricultural produce and foodstuffs. All these problems are quite sensitive for Russia in terms of both improving the structure of its industry and maintaining employment at a proper level. Of special concern is Russian agriculture that has got stuck for the time being between the past and the future, and still badly needs government support and protection from stiff competition. To adapt its legislation to WTO requirements Russia will have to alter about a hundred laws and over four hundred regulations.

There are therefore quite a few objective factors that do not enable Russia to accept all the demands of its trade partners. Compromises need to be sought, and this takes time and effort. But delaying Russian entry into WTO is also fraught with undesirable consequences. The Russian government supposes that the main part of negotiations may be finished by the end of 2002, and that accession will take place in 2003 or 2004.[110]

Financial relations

An important component of economic partnership between Russia and the EU is their **investment co-operation**. Conditions for such co-operation are less favourable than for trade in goods and services. It has been impeded by the investment climate that is still inadequate in Russia. Economic instability, the lack of a solid legal basis, criminalisation of business and the arbitrary rule of corrupt officials are the main obstacles to foreign investment. Under these circumstances, foreign companies are apprehensive about investing their money in Russia's economy, especially as regards long-term investments. It comes as no surprise that accumulated direct foreign investment per person living in Russia did not exceed $136 in 1999, whereas the corresponding figure for China was $241, for Poland $776, and for Hungary as much as $1,896.[111]

Nevertheless, the total amount of foreign capital attracted to Russia grew almost steadily over the years of reforms (see Table 3.3). An understandable disturbance occurred only in 1998-99; but in 2000 the situation began to improve again.

When considering the composition of foreign investment, it should be kept in mind that in Russia *direct* investment includes not only an investor's financial resources but also material assets (including machinery, equipment, semi-finished products, technology and licences), and even services (building and assembly work) whose total share in joint stock capital is no less than 10 per cent. *Portfolio* investment implies acquisition of shares within 10 per cent of an enterprise's joint stock capital and purchase of its bonds, bills and other securities. According to World Bank estimates, the amount of portfolio investment in Russia has been understated by the State Statistics Committee by three to four times. *Other* investment includes investment in government securities and long-term private credits granted by banks, exporters, etc.

Table 3.3: The amount and composition of foreign investment in Russia, 1991-2000 ($ billion)

	1993	1994	1995	1996	1997	1998	1999	2000
Total	2.92	1.05	2.98	6.97	12.37	11.77	9.56	10.96
Direct	2.57	0.55	2.02	2.43	5.39	3.36	4.26	4.43
From EU	n a	n a	0.34	0.73	2.08	2.10	2.95	n a
Portfolio	0.07	0.00	0.04	0.13	0.70	0.19	0.03	0.15
Other	0.28	0.50	0.92	4.41	6.28	8.22	5.27	6.38

Sources: State Statistics Committee; Eurostat (COMEXT, CROWOS), June 2001.

As Table 3.3 shows, 'other' investment was growing most rapidly in 1994-98 and, in 1996-98, far exceeded direct investment, because GKOs/OFZs were specially attractive. After the financial crisis the situation changed radically: the share of capital investment in the financial, banking and insurance sectors fell from 59 per cent in 1997 to 20 per cent in 1998 and to 3 per cent in 1999, while the share of investment in industry rose from 32 per cent to 40 per cent and to 51 per cent, respectively; and in 2000 it was 43 per cent.[112]

The chief foreign investors are West European countries and the USA. By the end of 2000, West European countries accounted for more than 70 per cent of $32 billion in accumulated foreign investment in Russia, though the USA is significantly ahead of them in direct investment.

The inflow of direct foreign investment in Russia is far from meeting its needs. No less than $4-5 billion is needed annually for modernisation and further development of Russia's telecommunications alone. The government-approved project for further development of the oil and gas industry until 2005 provides for attracting $4 billion of foreign capital a year. In the view of the World Bank, no less than $60 billion needs to be invested in the next ten years in the electric power industry. Meanwhile, in 1994, direct foreign investment in Russia did not exceed 0.2 per cent of its GDP, in 1995-96 it was about 0.6 per cent, in 1997 1.4 per cent, in 1998 1 per cent, and in 1999 1.1 per cent. (In comparison: the inflow of such investment in France in 1999 was 2.8 per cent of its GDP, in Hungary 4 per cent, in Poland 4.9 per cent and in the United Kingdom 6 per cent.)[113]

This has been due, as we saw, to the investment climate that is still not investor-friendly in Russia. According to data in the *Financial Times*, as regards attractiveness for investors in 2000 the country was only in the 32nd place (though in 1999 it was 49th). Apart from economic instability, criminalisation of business and corruption of officials, foreign investors are deterred by the lack of a solid and well-thought-out legal basis. The Russian leadership has repeatedly announced its intention to extend the national legal regime to non-residents. This principle was written into the 1991 law 'On Foreign Investment in the Russian Federation'. World experience shows, however, that granting the national regime to non-residents is effective only in developed countries with a stable investor-friendly climate. In those countries where the regime does not provide this, additional incentives are needed for attracting non-residents' capital to certain regions or industries that are of vital importance at a given stage of development.

In Russia this problem, which is common for the economies in transition, has been compounded by two circumstances. First, there was the Left majority in the Duma till 2000 that was constantly impeding liberalisation of capital imports on the pretext that foreigners will 'buy up' Russia's industry, 'enslave' the country, etc. Powerful pressure on the government and the Duma by Russia's largest companies (above all, fuel and raw material companies) that are not interested in the appearance of foreign competitors within the country must also be taken into account. So access to some sectors of Russia's economy is still closed to non-residents, or restrictions are still in force on the share of foreigners in joint stock capital.

Secondly, with Russian industry in an acute structural crisis, special measures are needed to attract foreign investment into some branches of manufacturing. If such measures are not taken, investment in the real sector of Russia's economy will be channelled, as before, to those industries where a handsome profit can be yielded without great effort, by-passing less profitable industries that are of strategic importance for Russia's future. By mid-1999, out of total accumulated direct foreign investment, 20 per cent was invested in the food industry, 19 per cent in communications facilities, 18 per cent in the fuel industry, 10 per cent in trade, and only 4 per cent in machine building.[114] Such a situation cannot be changed without a flexible system of preferential terms for non-residents.

Russian lawmakers have been confronted with a threefold task: first, to improve the national economic regime in order to reduce to a minimum the list of activities subject to licensing (it still includes more than 200 types of activity), to make procedures for organising tenders and for other forms of foreigners' access transparent, to simplify the existing tax system, to strengthen legal guarantees for investors, etc.; secondly, to enlarge the number of non-residents to whom this national regime is to be spread, and to reduce restrictions on the inflow of foreign capital in Russia to reasonable limits; thirdly, to improve the existing system of preferential terms for non-resident investors at the federal and regional levels in order to make it more flexible and, at the same time, to exclude from the system those Russian investors that transfer their savings to offshore funds and then repatriate capital under the guise of 'foreign' capital.

There has already been some progress in these areas. The law of 9 July 1999 'On Foreign Investment' provides for a number of important guarantees for investors, including: the right of foreign investors to acquire real estate and lease plots of land; compensation for losses incurred by an investor as a result of unlawful actions committed by government agencies or their officials;

against nationalisation, requisition and other forms of confiscation of property; the right to use revenues and profits made in the territory of Russia; and unrestricted repatriation of property, information, etc. that had been brought into the country earlier. Worth special mention is an important guarantee against unfavourable changes in national legislation through the entire period of recoupment of an investment project (the so-called stabilisation or 'grandfather' clause). True, a quite narrow interpretation of this clause is given in the law. But an especially important step towards improvement in the investment climate both for the domestic and foreign entrepreneurs may have been the law adopted in summer 2001, which brings down the rate of tax on profits from 35 per cent to 24 per cent. In this regard Russia is becoming one of only a few countries with such easy-term tax regulations.

Exxon's decision to proceed with the vast Sakhalin project shows that the steps to improve conditions for investors have had some effect. However, much has still to be done to improve the investment climate in Russia: in particular, to extend the force of the law 'On Foreign Investment in the Russian Federation' to the banking and insurance sectors where other and less investor-friendly norms are still in effect; to radically simplify procedures for registration of enterprises where foreign capital has a stake; to shorten the list of types of non-resident investors' activities subject to licensing, etc.

Apart from domestic legislation, international regulations for investment also play an important part in attracting direct foreign investment. By the end of 2000, Russia had 53 bilateral agreements on encouragement to and reciprocal protection of foreign investment, including those with all the EU countries, with Canada and the USA, and with eleven Central and East European countries. It also acceded to the 1965 Washington convention on procedures for settlement of investment disputes, the 1985 Seoul convention on the establishment of an international agency for investment guarantees, though a few steps remain to complete ratification of the European Energy Charter.

The rate, scope and composition of investment in the Russian economy depend not only on the investment climate but also on the efficiency of Russia's credit and banking system that has to accumulate savings and transform them into capital investment. It should be borne in mind that

Russia, lacking a market for investment capital in the Anglo-American sense, will have to rely, at least for some time to come, on investment banking in what has been the German tradition. After the August 1998 financial tempest that devastated a part of Russia's banking infrastructure, it is being gradually restored (see Figure 2.7 on p.53). But in the scale of its provision of credits to the national economy, it lags far behind the banking systems of Western Europe. The assets of all banks of Russia in 1993-99 did not exceed, on average, 29 per cent of GDP, whereas in Germany the ratio in 1995 was 50 per cent, in the USA 59 per cent, in France 91 per cent and in Britain as much as 233 per cent.[115]

But the main problem of Russia's banking system consists not so much in the paucity of its financial resources as in its structural weakness. Most Russian banks are small or medium-sized institutions that proved to be more resistant to financial turbulence than large banks. But they are much less competitive and unable to emulate strong domestic and foreign banks. The main thing to note here is that they are not able to provide large long-term investment credits.

Immediately after the crisis, the Central Bank of Russia (CBR) concentrated its efforts on tackling two, not simple, tasks aimed at restructuring the banking sphere. On the one hand, the task was to liquidate or restore Moscow's insolvent large banks that had been hardest hit by the financial crisis. In the spring of 1999, the state Agency for Restructuring Credit Institutions (ARKO) also became involved in this work. The Agency was set up following the example of similar agencies established in a number of South East Asian countries that had been hit by the crisis. A number of Russian banks that were among the largest in the past are still suspended. On the other hand, the CBR has been monitoring the activities of all other banks more thoroughly, revoking the licences of unreliable banks, increasing the minimum assets required, and pressing for greater transparency of their activities. At the same time, the ARKO has been helping to restore the capacity of regional banks that suffered much less from the crisis.

All of this has contributed to a consolidation of Russian banks. From September 1998 to February 2001, there were 22 mergers involving 48 banks;

and in May 2001, the Moscow International Bank and the Austria Bank, both of which are quite big, merged.[116]

The government for its part has been trying to improve the legal basis of the banking sector. In June 2000, the government's plan of action in the area of social policy and economic modernisation for 2000-2001 was approved. The plan specifies the main tasks aiming to improve the financial infrastructure: banking sector, stock market, investment funds and insurance services. The purpose is to provide for legal mechanisms to be developed for carrying out bankruptcy proceedings against unviable banks; improve the system of taxation of credit institutions; introduce international standards of bank supervision and greater transparency of banking business; and create conditions for converting credit institutions to international accounting standards.

Of no small importance among such measures is legal support for conditions conducive to an inflow of foreign capital into Russia's banking business. From 1993 to 1996, the share of non-residents in this kind of business was limited to 12 per cent. However, in conditions of economic and legal instability, foreign banks have not shown much interest in Russia's credit market. By April 2001, there were only 116 banks in Russia with a share of foreign capital, including 27 banks with a foreign stake of 100 per cent. To rectify such a state of affairs, much has still to be done in terms of law and organisationally.

In this context, recommendations by the IMF and the European Bank of Reconstruction and Development (EBRD) are of some help to Russia. But successful transformation of the banking system depends above all on the effectiveness of measures taken by the government and on its ability to find a common language with the Duma.

The other sectors of Russia's financial infrastructure - **the stock market, investment institutions and insurance companies** - have been developed to a still lesser extent than banks. As regards the amount of assets and investment, Russia's insurance companies are next to commercial banks. Over the period 1992-98, more than 2,000 such companies of various kinds were set up in Russia. They invest their financial resources in government securities, in the shares of private companies, in real estate, etc. After the crisis their number dwindled by more than a quarter but now many of them have already restored their positions. According to the assessment made by The Economist Intelligence Unit, 'the sector has great long-term promise, as Russia is seriously underinsured at present, but the pace of development will depend largely on the government's handling of the outstanding legal and regulatory issues facing the sector. Progress will be slow unless the industry can persuade the authorities to attach a higher priority to its needs.'[117]

The country's first ever stock exchange appeared in Moscow in 1991, to be followed by stock exchanges that were established in many regions of Russia; and purchase and sale of shares on the stock market was growing faster than changes were made in appropriate laws protecting the interests of the shareholders. The stock market developed, for the most part, through servicing the process of privatisation and redistribution of property after privatisation, as well as stock-jobbing. As regards its main function - accumulation of investment resources and making them accessible to enterprises - the stock market was performing it to only a minimal extent. So by 1997, out of more than 50,000 open joint-stock companies that had been registered, only around 150 had a market quotation. By then, capitalisation of Russia's stock market accounted for only 12 per cent of GDP, which is much lower than in many developed countries.[118]

The 1998 financial crisis dealt a heavy blow to Russia's securities market. But the potential for its restoration and development is quite considerable. Putting this potential into effect has, however, been restrained by big gaps and contradictions that still exist in legislation, and by state agencies' lax control over the implementation of laws and decrees that have already been adopted.

Technical assistance

Future prospects for economic interaction and further development of cultural, humanitarian and other ties between Russia and the EU depend to no small degree on how rapidly and successfully reform of Russia's economic and political systems will be completed and on how far they will be drawn nearer to West European systems. The programme 'Technical Assistance to the

Commonwealth of Independent States' (Tacis) is called upon to facilitate and accelerate this process of convergence. It was conceived in December 1990 as an equivalent of the Phare programme of technical assistance to the countries of Central and Eastern Europe and began to be implemented in 1991. At first, this assistance was destined for the Soviet Union as a whole, and since 1992 for twelve former Soviet republics. Because of the scale of Russia and its needs for assistance, a significant (though far from proportional to this scale) part of financing falls to Russia.

Under an indicative programme for 1996-99, the priority areas of technical assistance to Russia were human resources development, social protection, energy, environment, food and agriculture. Altogether, as part of Tacis programmes intended for Russia, 779 projects were carried out, or are being implemented, or are at the stage of preparation, with four-fifths of all those carried out before 1997 having proved to be successful. Apart from this, various special sub-programmes were or are being implemented. Such an extensive and diversified aid, including the training of Russian specialists, consultations in drawing up standards, specific industrial, agricultural, transport and telecommunication projects, assistance to development of small and medium-sized enterprises, has been of benefit to Russia. Technical assistance has also been provided at a supranational level: the CIS Interstate programme; programme for nuclear safety; and programme of co-operation in border areas. A significant part of assistance under these programmes also falls to Russia and, in the opinion of the European Commission, is successful.

True, the Tacis-financed projects have been implemented, for the most part, by specialists from EU countries. Until recently, nearly 80 per cent of allocated funds were spent on services provided by organisations and experts of the European Union.[119] Participation of Russian organisations in drawing up projects and in implementing them has been unjustifiably limited. Moreover, Russia has quite often obtained financial resources for implementation of specific projects after a long delay (almost a year and a half after the date of submitting an application). This made itself felt especially strongly in the period of the 1998 financial crisis when provision of technical assistance in due time could have appreciably alleviated its aftermath.

These and other shortcomings of the mechanism for providing technical assistance were removed, in part, in the new Regulations of the programme for 2000-06. Rules and procedures for obtaining financial resources have been simplified significantly, there is now a bigger participation of the Russian side in drawing up and implementing specific projects, and the focus is shifting from advice provided by consultants to the training of Russian specialists. What is most important is that a quarter of annual financing will be directed towards encouraging foreign investment in Russia. It is the first time that provision has been made for financing projects of industrial co-operation between Russian and EU enterprises. At the same time, assistance continues to be given to the implementation of the government's programme of market-economy based reforms (in 2000, 42 per cent of total allocations were earmarked for this purpose), to helping ensure nuclear safety (37 per cent of the sum total), and for other purposes.

In addition, an agreement on scientific and technical co-operation was concluded between the EU and Russia in November 2000. It encompasses a wide range of scientific and technical interaction in environmental protection, health services, agriculture, industrial technologies, transport and communications. Thus the Information and Training Centre for space technologies was inaugurated in Moscow in January 2001. The task of the Centre is not only to train Russian specialists but also to draw up procedures for certification of the space equipment of the EU and Russia, with far-reaching aims pursued.

All of this is raising hopes for greater efficiency of the EU's technical assistance to Russia.

Enlargement of the EU and Nato, and Russia's interests

The impending entry of seven countries of Central and Eastern Europe (CEE), three Baltic countries, Cyprus and Malta into the EU will undoubtedly alter the existing balance of advantages and disadvantages in economic relations between Russia and the European Union. In 1998-99, these twelve countries accounted, on average, for 14.8 per cent of total Russian exports and 7.3 per cent of imports.[120] Russia exports to these countries the same amount of goods as it exports to eleven 'near-abroad' countries of the CIS, though less than half of what it exports to the fifteen countries of the EU. The incorporation of this foreign market that is quite important for Russia into the single EU market may have twofold consequences for the country.

On the one hand, after the entry of the new states into the European Union, the provisions of the Partnership and Co-operation Agreement between the Russian Federation and the EU will be extended to them and as a result, in a number of respects, conditions will become more favourable than they are now for Russian exports to their markets. First, the common tariff of the EU is appreciably lower than the national tariffs of the candidate countries. According to estimates by the United Nations Economic Commission for Europe, this difference is an average of 12 percentage points in favour of Russian exporters of minerals, 15 for textiles, 18 for machines and chemicals, 21 for timber and ferrous metals, and 23 percentage points for petroleum products.[121] Besides, the EU applies quantitative restrictions on imports only in exceptional cases, whereas the candidate countries use them quite often.

Secondly, Russian exporters and importers are confronted in these countries with unwarranted and very often extortionate rates of transit payment. After their accession to the EU, this bacchanalia must give way to a uniform, predictable and civilised settlement of transit terms and conditions. Thirdly, the customs houses inherited from the recent past that are still under-equipped for border crossings, especially in the Baltic states, leave wide scope for smuggling and other customs violations, causing no small loss of revenue for Russia. As a condition of joining the EU, they will have to upgrade their customs houses to meet its high standards. Fourthly, should conflict situations arise, Russian companies will be able to protect their interests within the EU's unified and precisely defined field of law rather than in present-day legal regimes that are of different calibre and are not entirely civilised.

On the other hand, the incorporation of the Central and East European and Baltic countries into the single market of the European Union is also fraught with negative consequences for Russia. The main one is gradual replacement of the former technical standards, to which Russian exporters have got accustomed since the CMEA times, by new ones. This will place additional barriers in the way of Russia's traditional supplies to the Central and East European and Baltic countries: of machinery, industrial equipment, chemicals, textiles and some foodstuffs. True, Russia too is going to switch over to all-European standards, but it is quite a long process.

Russian exporters and importers of agricultural products will also be confronted with serious problems. Exports to these countries will be faced by higher barriers that protect the EU's single agricultural market. Imports from them will be significantly complicated by an inevitable rise in their domestic prices that will have to be raised to the quite high level of prices within the EU's single agricultural market. So Russia will be deprived of supplies of agricultural products at comparatively low prices from Hungary, Poland, Bulgaria and other Central and East European countries, at least if the Union cuts back its export subsidies following agreement in the WTO.

It is not to be excluded either that there will be a more extensive application of anti-dumping proceedings against Russian exporters, and that Russia's losses will consequently be greater. Finally, many transit and other problems will arise concerning the Kaliningrad Oblast when it becomes an enclave within the economic and political space of the EU.

All these problems are of serious concern to Moscow, but have been treated with understanding in Brussels. To ease a potential complication of economic relations between Russia and the EU, the parties established in the summer of 2000 a special working group to discuss all aspects related to the EU's enlargement that are causing anxiety in Russia. But taken a whole, the upcoming enlargement has met with quite a calm reaction in Moscow.

Russia has reacted quite differently to **Nato's eastward expansion**; and it is as well that a western readership should understand how the enlargement of Nato, combined with western attitudes to the Chechnya wars, has appeared to many Russians, and to this writer in particular. Thus Russia and the West ceased to be 'potential adversaries' from the time when it became clear that in case of a military conflict they would inevitably have destroyed each other and there would have been no one to emerge as a victor. A potential and even real threat to peace comes today from Islamic extremism that sees no other way to spread its influence but a jihad in the name of Allah, and from some dictatorial regimes in developing countries (for instance, Iraq). This threat has been intensified because technologies for the production of chemical, bacteriological and even nuclear weapons are becoming ever more accessible to developing countries as they mature technologically. Such a situation, as well as combat against international terrorism, drug trafficking and other forms of crime, calls for concerted effort of the civilised states of the world community and for the creation of a single security space common for all at the Euro-Atlantic level. And Russia is ready for far-reaching co-operation in this field with both the EU and the USA. An important step in this direction was taken at the EU-Russia Summit in October 2001, which decided on monthly meetings at political level between representatives of Russia and of the EU Political and Security Committee on the subject of crisis prevention and management and confirmed that arrangements would be made for 'possible Russian participation in (the EU's) civilian and military crisis-management operations'.[122]

However, the forms of pooling such efforts leave much to be desired. After all, the West has still not sufficiently adapted to the new circumstances the Nato military organisation that was established at a quite different time for the solution of quite different tasks. That form of organisation was then fully natural and justified. But after the end of the Cold War its old structure become inappropriate for the new tasks. The tragic events in the USA in September 2001 demonstrated that the enemy is no longer where western strategy was accustomed to see it, and that Nato is not able to defend its members against attack by this new enemy.

In the light of the above, an enlargement of Nato has appeared to be an unsafe process, moved by force of inertia. The process arose because some influential political forces were not prepared to take a fresh view of the world and give up thinking in obsolete military clichés.

While not corresponding to present-day military and political realities, Nato's enlargement has caused additional tensions in relations between Russia and the EU. It is clear to any objective person who follows current events that without proper interaction with Russia it is impossible to ensure security within the Euro-Atlantic space. But it is also clear that inclusion of the CEE and Baltic countries into Nato, which was originally targeted against Russia, and bringing Nato's military infrastructure right up to Russia's borders, could not but cause anxiety among Russia's political and military circles and thus provoke them to take adequate protective measures.

Another aspect of political tensions between Russia and the EU stems from events in Chechnya that turned in recent years into a breeding ground for counterfeiters, drug traffickers and slave traders, and into a centre for training terrorists who operate not only in Russia but also in other regions. With a growing rate of international crime world-wide, including in Europe, and in the context of joint security policy being shaped in the EU, it would be understandable if European Union leaders were concerned about the fact that, apart from breeding grounds for international crime in the Arab East, in Latin America and some other faraway regions of the world, a new locus of this severe disease appeared in the south-eastern corner of Europe - in the Northern Caucasus. Claims that Russia did not prevent such a disease from appearing in its territory would be justified and natural. But, however strange it might be, complaints of a quite different kind were lodged against Russia. It was accused of inadequately humane measures against this contagion that poses a danger to all of Europe. What is more, the complaints were exaggerated and hypocritical.

When Chechnya started in the early 1990s to develop rapidly into a territory where no norms of law except the law of force are valid; when mediaeval practices of abduction of people and making them slaves began to flourish there; when nearly 300,000 refugees who are not Chechens left Chechnya as their life there became unbearable, neither the EU nor the West as a whole showed the least concern over violation of human rights there, considering it an 'internal Russian problem'. When, in August 1999, well-armed Chechen bandits intruded into neighbouring Dagestan in the hope of kindling a flame of 'war of liberation' and began to blow up apartment buildings in Moscow and other Russian cities at night, the West remained indifferent.

But as soon as Russia began to smash successfully first in Dagestan and then in Chechnya the army of many thousands of Chechen bandits and of mercenaries from other countries fighting on their side, the EU immediately called upon Moscow not to use 'excessive military force', began to accuse it of a deliberate escalation of military operations and even temporarily suspended implementation of the Tacis programme. When in response to Arab terrorists' assaults, Israel unleashed powerful missile and bomb strikes, killing not only gunmen but also civilians in Lebanon, the EU closed its eyes. But when Russia (by the way, not in a foreign territory but in its own) did the same, it was indignantly condemned as an improper use of force. Against the backdrop of recent massive bombings of Serbia by Nato aircraft, such condemnation appeared to be especially hypocritical.

Then, when the military part of the operation to destroy a most dangerous seat of international terrorism was over and the remaining terrorists unleashed mine warfare, the EU continued to accuse Russia of violating human rights, disregarding the fact that not only Russian servicemen but also many civilian residents are killed every day by bombs planted by terrorists, that gunmen time and again kill Chechen administrators, who try to restore peaceful life in their towns and villages, and even murder imams. Evidently some West European policy makers have not considered the impact of such murders on citizens' rights. They were concerned only about violations committed by Russian servicemen in operations against terrorists and murderers. This gave grounds for Russians, the overwhelming majority of whom support the government's policy in Chechnya, to suspect that Western leaders were concerned, not about human rights, but about quite different problems that seem to be within the sphere of geopolitics.

It appears, however, that the dreadful demonstration of the terrorist menace on 11 September 2001, followed by Russia's very co-operative attitude towards the international response, may lead to greater western understanding of Russia's problem regarding Chechnya and a historic shift in its relationship with Nato and with the United States.

The EU is Russia's chief strategic partner

For more than three centuries now Western Europe has been Russia's chief economic and political partner. Its importance in this capacity is growing still more as new Central and East European countries are incorporated into the EU. This integrated organism will develop in the next few years into a powerful geo-economic and geo-political centre equal in the force of its influence to the USA and surpassing Japan and China. Notwithstanding statements by many Russian policy makers that the interests of Russia lie equally in both the West and the East, the scale is being clearly tipped in favour of the West, or to be more precise, in favour of the European Union.

Economically, at this stage Russia and the EU successfully complement each other as trade partners. Russian supplies meet 16 per cent of the European Union's import requirements for oil, 20 per cent for natural gas and a substantial part of its needs for non-ferrous metals, timber and other basic resources. Russia in turn is very interested in receiving from the EU countries machinery and other investment goods for the restoration and modernisation of its industry. Evidence of mutual interest in such a division of labour was the Russian-EU summit held at the end of October 2000, where the West European side, with world oil prices standing high and with regard to consequences ensuing from the burning of liquid fuel for the environment, expressed the desire to increase its imports of Russian gas and electric power. The EU is ready to encourage the involvement of its companies in expanding production of natural gas and other energy resources in Russia at all stages - from exploration and development of fields up to and including development of transport infrastructure. That means investing several tens of billions of dollars. Russia, in its turn, intends to strive for a joint long-term energy policy with a view to forming a single European and, in future, Eurasian energy space.

With an acute shortage of investment resources, such a partnership is certainly beneficial to Russia. But in the final analysis it will put Russia into a situation when it actually has the status of a fuel and raw material appendage of Western Europe and, what is more, will reinforce the dangerous distortion of the sectoral structure of industry. It is dangerous not only in the short and medium term but also in a more distant future because it engenders the so-called 'Dutch disease': exaggerated development of a narrow group of export-oriented sectors of the national economy to the detriment of the other sectors that decay and become degraded. The symptoms of this disease with which

Russia's economy is afflicted are quite obvious: in recent years the lion's share of export revenues has been invested in the fuel and energy complex, in non-ferrous and ferrous metallurgy, whereas manufacturers have curtailed their high-tech production sectors that are most important from the standpoint of the strategy of adjusting Russia to fit in with the world economy.

It is clear that Russia, which still has a big scientific and technical potential, skilled personnel, and the latest technologies in some sectors, cannot rest content with the continuation of such a tendency. The fundamental task for Russia's leadership is to make use of the country's present-day comparative advantage in the power industry, metallurgy and some other basic industries for the accumulation of financial resources and their redistribution in favour of promising high-tech production sectors and for support of the Russian scientific and technical potential. In this context, investment by EU companies in Russia's machine building can have a big part to play. Here, it would be useful to draw up a joint package of measures aimed at attracting West European investment in the Russian economy, and make round-table discussions, in which industrialists and entrepreneurs of Russia and the EU participate, more active.

Expanded co-operation between Russian and West European scientists can also have an important part to play. Over the four years of its existence, the International Association for Assistance to Co-operation of Scientists from the CIS countries (INTAC) initiated more than 1,200 research projects, involving nearly 12,000 Russian scientists and the same number of West European scientists in physics, mathematics, telecommunications, information technologies, ecology, power engineering, astronautics, social sciences and humanities. The Agreement on Co-operation in Science and Technology, signed at the end of 2000, is to help promote this mutually beneficial co-operation.

As regards organisational forms of economic interaction between Russia and the EU, they depend largely on when and how successfully Russia will cope with the above-mentioned fundamental task. So far, the legal and institutional framework laid down in the PCA has suited Russia perfectly. But till now the opportunities afforded by this agreement encompassing a wide range of areas have not been fully used.

One such opportunity declared in the PCA - the future establishment of a free trade area - is worth dwelling upon in more detail. The proposal to consider the possibility of establishing it came from Russia. An expert group set up for this purpose in March 2000 at the insistence of Moscow submitted a report recommending postponement of negotiations on this subject until Russia fulfils three preliminary conditions. First it should join the WTO and undertake appropriate obligations for liberalising the existing trade regime. Secondly, it should completely fulfil its obligations under the Partnership and Co-operation Agreement with the EU. Thirdly, it should be ready to make changes in its trade regulations and appropriate procedures so as to get properly prepared, which will not be easy, for the conditions of free competition in such a free trade area. The European Commission agreed that negotiations on the subject now would be premature and also expressed the hope that the support being provided by the EU for economic, structural and legal reforms in Russia would, in due course, make prospects for a free trade area more realistic.[123]

Harsh reality stands behind this diplomatic wording. The difficulties with which Russia has been confronted, when opening up its economy, and the structural, institutional and macroeconomic problems that still remain unsolved within the country make the establishment of a free trade area between Russia and the EU quite problematic, at least in the next few years. A great difference in the level of competitiveness of Russian and West European goods and services should not be overlooked either. According to the 'Global Competitiveness Report 2000', prepared for the World Economic Forum, Germany comes third among 58 countries with respect to the competitiveness index, the Netherlands fourth, Sweden seventh and Britain eighth, while Russia is placed 52nd.[124]

If Russian import barriers are removed and free trade is introduced, Western exporters will have far greater chances to push aside producers on Russia's domestic market than Russian exporters to do the same in the EU's single market. For Russia the benefits of a free trade area, taken as a whole, will be outweighed by serious losses. To all appearances, much time will pass after Russia's entry into the WTO before the establishment of such a zone will become safe and acceptable for the country. But another outcome is possible. It should not be forgotten that the idea, which emerged in 1998, of a transatlantic free trade area even between trade and economic partners of equivalent weight - the USA and the EU - quietly died of natural causes. The same outcome is not to be excluded in the case in point.

The future of economic relations between these two centres of gravity in Europe is to be viewed precisely as partnership, diversified and mutually beneficial, but with them standing at a respectable distance from each other. After all, there is a very big difference in their present-day economic position, in their geo-economic and geo-political interests, and in their priorities not only today but in future as well. Even given their very active economic, scientific and technical co-operation, the most probable model of their interrelationships is a model of a 'dumb-bell': two weighty parts of Eurasia connected with each other by a more or less firm handle.

Further development and deepening of **political partnership** between Russia and the EU appears to be far more realistic. Both parties are still more concerned over European security problems. These problems have become especially topical in light of the recent tragedy in Kosovo, current events in Macedonia and the threat, posed by Islamic extremists, drug traffickers and other criminal elements, that comes from Afghanistan, Pakistan and some countries of the Middle East, highlighted by the terrorist attacks of September 2001. Both the European Union and Russia have, in Winston Churchill's words, their 'soft underbellies'. For the former, they are the Balkans, and for the latter, Central Asia. But European security cannot be divided into 'ours' and 'yours'. It depends now, as never before, on an agreed strategy of these two main European partners.

Whereas in the economic sphere these partners are not of equal weight and their priorities do not always coincide, they are generally very close to each other in regard to all-European security and global stability. There is a long list of priorities that coincide in this area: from non-proliferation of mass destruction weapons to settlement of regional conflicts in Europe and in areas in its immediate proximity; from combat against international terrorism to eradication of drug trafficking and white-slave traffic; from restriction of illegal migration to crackdown on money laundering.

A weak interaction until now between Russia and the EU in these spheres is largely explained by the fact that it was only fairly recently given competences in the fields of foreign policy, defence, security, and police and judicial co-operation. Common policies in these fields are, moreover, in a number of aspects still in a transitional state and have not yet crystallised. Russia is ready for the closest co-operation in all these areas. Its aim is to help promote strategic partnership with the EU in order to build a stable and balanced security architecture in Europe, for peace and openness in this continent. The 'Medium-term Strategy for Development of Relations between the Russian Federation and the European Union (2000-2010)' emphasised in particular Moscow's intention 'to work out Russia's position on the 'defence identity' of the European Union with the Western European Union to be included in it, as well as to develop political and military contacts with the WEU as an integral part of the EU, and to promote practical co-operation in the area of security (peace-making, crisis settlement, various aspects of arms limitation and reduction, etc.).'[125]

Among the questions that should not be ignored are Washington's questionable plans to revise the foundations of existing agreements on anti-missile defence; stable development in the Central and East European and Baltic countries; joint concern for an all-European balance of forces; and prevention of detriment to Russia resulting from the EU's enlargement, including in particular settlement of transit, visa and other problems related to the Kaliningrad region.

For the implementation of these tasks, organisational forms have already been established under the PCA: the Council for Co-operation at the level of foreign ministers, the Committee for Co-operation at the level of senior officials, and the Committee for Parliamentary Co-operation. Regular political dialogue at all these levels, together with the biannual Summit meetings, is now the most advanced sphere of interaction between Russia and the EU. What is really important is that within the framework of this dialogue the parties should consider not so much the problems concerning conflict situations that have already arisen as measures to prevent them. Some such measures are considered in the following chapter.

Chapter 4:
The Union's Common
Strategy on Russia

John Pinder

The Union's most effective instruments for its external policy are still those in the economic field. But during the past decade it has done much to develop other aspects of external policy, with the common foreign and security policy (CFSP) and more recently the European security and defence policy (ESDP), along with the move towards enlargement to Central and Eastern Europe and the international negotiations on climate change. These are all significant for EU-Russia relations. But because they are work in progress, there are often expectations that the Union can deliver more in these fields than it is capable of doing; and this can lead to scepticism about its ability to improve its capacity for effective action, which past experience shows it is often able to do. So it may be useful to recall briefly how the Community, now the Union, has developed in this field and where further development may be needed if it is to accomplish such things as the building of a strong partnership with Russia.

It was the aggressive stance of the Soviet Union that led to the project for a European army, which foundered in 1954 when the French National Assembly failed to ratify the European Defence Community Treaty. While the member states went on to establish the European Economic Community, defence became a no-go area for the Community until the Maastricht Treaty came into force in 1993. Attempts to provide for effective co-operation in other aspects of foreign policy were also impeded as France, together with

Britain after it joined the Community in 1973, would not accept the Community as a framework for developing a common foreign policy.

Development of the common foreign and security policy

The European Political Co-operation (EPC) procedures for foreign policy co-operation were initiated in 1970, responding to French fears that the Community would be diluted by the forthcoming accession of a sceptical Britain. But the French themselves weakened the EPC by insisting that it be purely intergovernmental and separate from the Community. Although in the 1980s the Single European Act brought it closer to the Community, the EPC's achievements were limited largely to issuing joint declarations and accustoming member states' diplomats to working together on foreign policy. It had little impact on policy towards the Soviet Union, with one significant exception, when an EPC initiative secured a place for human rights on the agenda of the Conference on Security and Co-operation in Europe. In 1975 a commitment to respect them was included in the Helsinki Final Act, whose signatories included the Soviet Union; and this made some contribution to the ferment in Central and Eastern Europe and also in Russia that became a factor in the dissolution of the Soviet system.

It was again, as in the 1950s, the action of the Soviet Union that caused the Community to envisage a new stage of co-operation in foreign and security policy, but this time in a very different way. In place of its earlier expansionary policy, Gorbachev led the Soviet Union to withdraw its troops from Central and Eastern Europe; and this opened the way to unification of Germany's western and eastern parts. But France, as an occupying power under the post-war settlement, had a decisive influence over German unification, which President Mitterrand was not willing to accept without integrating Germany yet more firmly in the European Community. One element in this policy was the single currency, to make the economic integration more complete. The other was a common foreign and security policy, aiming to ensure that Germany would not use its greater size and new-found freedom of manoeuvre to pursue an independent policy towards its eastern neighbours, to the detriment of France and other partners in the West. Chancellor Kohl, for whom, as for many among the German political establishment, a federal Europe was a desirable goal, gladly accepted both; and they became central features of the Maastricht Treaty.

Maastricht provided for a CFSP that did not differ greatly in substance from the EPC but had more ambitious aims, greater political will behind it and openings for further development. It was established as a second pillar of what was to be called the European Union, alongside the central, Community pillar. It provided for 'joint actions', within the scope of which decisions could be taken by qualified majority, but only if this procedure had been unanimously accepted when it was decided to undertake the joint action in question. This convoluted procedure could hardly be expected to lead to a practice of majority voting. It was, rather, an indication that a number of member states, including Germany, had wanted the CFSP to be located within the Community and favoured the introduction of qualified majority voting, while Britain, France and some others did not. The Treaty also mentioned a 'common defence policy', and even 'a common defence', but in equivocal terms that reflected a stand-off between the French, who wanted to develop a European defence capacity, and the British, who did not for fear it would undermine Nato.

Russia was involved in two of the first four joint actions. In 1993 the Union supplied administrators and monitors for Russia's parliamentary elections; and the French initiative to help stabilise Eastern Europe by diplomatic means was adopted as a joint action, which culminated with a conference in Paris in March 1995 when over fifty states agreed on a Stability Pact for Europe.

Stability did not extend to the West Balkans, however, where the wars erupted in 1991 and continued through most of the decade. The EU has made the major contribution to reconstruction and civilian peace-keeping, for example monitoring elections, deploying and training police, assisting institution-building and supplying aid of around €1 billion a year. The British and French have also provided the largest contingents of troops in Bosnia. But through the 1990s, the Europeans were strikingly dependent on the Americans in dealing with violent conflict and the diplomacy associated with it; and this led to a loss of confidence in the CFSP and to widespread disillusion with the Union. The declared objects of the CFSP had not been matched by institutions and instruments capable of achieving them, and governments became increasingly aware that improvements were required.

The Amsterdam Treaty, signed in June 1997 and in force in May 1999, introduced some significant changes. Instead of relying only on the shifting membership of the troika of current, preceding and succeeding Presidencies of the Council to represent the Union in matters pertaining to the CFSP, continuity was to be introduced by the appointment of a High Representative, who was also to be the Secretary-General of the Council Secretariat, to 'assist' the current President-in-Office with the task. The first incumbent, Javier Solana, was also appointed Secretary-General of Western European Union, which has been incorporated as the military organisation of the EU. His speech in Stockholm, cited at the beginning of the Introduction above, emphasised that high priority should be given to the EU's relations with Russia.

Another of the weaknesses of the CFSP that the Amsterdam Treaty sought to remedy was the lack of coherent policy planning. So a Policy Planning Unit was set up, located in the Council Secretariat and drawing staff from the Secretariat itself, member states, the WEU and the Commission.

The Amsterdam Treaty also introduced the concept of 'common strategies', intended to enhance the coherence of the decisions adopted in particular fields of activity of the CFSP. Here again, the Germans and others sought to enlarge the potential for majority voting in the CFSP; and the Treaty provided that common positions and joint actions within the scope of a common strategy could be decided by qualified majority. But a member state that opposes the majority can, 'for important and stated reasons of national policy', have the matter referred to the European Council, where it is to be settled by unanimous agreement. Not surprisingly, majority voting has hardly been employed, though obstructive behaviour may have been inhibited by its possible use. The first such strategy was the 'Common Strategy on Russia', agreed by the European Council under German Presidency in June 1999.

The Common Strategy has ambitious aims and assembles a comprehensive array of policies towards Russia. But apart from some of the economic policies which are based on the Community's institutions and common instruments, the CFSP is for the most part subject to weaker institutions and relies on the member states' co-operation in the use of their own instruments.

In March 2000 Chris Patten and Javier Solana presented a joint report to the European Council, drawing on the experience of the CFSP so far, particularly in the West Balkans.[126] They concluded that the unanimity procedure had led to action at the 'lowest common denominator' of the positions taken by the member states. While the states are not yet prepared to accept any majority decisions in the field of defence, several of them favour applying the procedure to matters that are not defence-related. Thus the Dutch government, during its Presidency of the Council in the run-up to the Maastricht Treaty, informed the Dutch parliament of its support for such a move.[127] Belgium, Germany and Italy have been steadily in favour; and they were joined by Austria and Luxembourg in the negotiations for the Amsterdam Treaty; France, Greece, Portugal and most particularly Britain were against.[128]

This position has been justified by the argument that it is not realistic to expect states in a minority to accept the decisions of a majority. But it is certainly not realistic to expect that aims such as those of the Common Strategy on Russia will be achievable, to the extent that decisions have to be taken unanimously; and it becomes increasingly implausible as the number of member states increases. A Declaration was appended to the Common Strategy on Russia, agreed under German Presidency, to the effect that 'the Council acts by qualified majority', presumably indicating agreement in principle that governments in a minority would refrain from referring a decision to be settled by unanimity in the European Council. There is some evidence that this has influenced behaviour in the Council on at least one occasion, when two member states had reservations about a joint action on a co-operation programme for non-proliferation and disarmament in Russia but chose to accept the view of the majority.[129] But that is not exactly a rich harvest. Readiness to accept a majority's view in a growing number of matters could have an important influence on the future success of the Common Strategy and, indeed, on the CFSP as a whole.

Apart from the voting procedure, the rotation of the Presidency every six months disturbs the evolution of the CFSP. Richard Holbrook, with his considerable experience as an American negotiator in the West Balkans, has drawn attention to the damage caused as each state, taking its turn in the chair, pursues a new priority.[130] The representatives of small states, moreover, who are often as well qualified as any to deal with the Union's internal affairs, may lack the knowledge and skills to handle the range of external matters under the CFSP.[131]

There has also been a tendency to keep the Commission understaffed for the tasks it should perform and to marginalise it from the CFSP, where its economic and environmental responsibilities are an essential component and, beyond that, it can apply its skills in identifying common interests. This behaviour has been at least in part due to the habit of member states' government machines to try to keep matters in their own hands and seek to cut the Commission down to size. But charged as they are to look after the interests of their own state, they are not well placed to identify and work for a general Union interest, as the Commission is constituted to do.

Patten and Solana also criticised the Union's decision-taking procedures as slow and unwieldy. They observed in particular that its budgetary procedures were too slow in responding to the rapidly developing needs of the CFSP, that the allocations in the EU's budget were inadequate and that member states had failed to pay their shares of the cost promptly. While there may have been some improvement since March 2000 when they presented their report, the development of the CFSP has remained work in progress that will not attain its full potential without further strengthening and reform.

The European security and defence policy

The principal developments in the Union's capacity to conduct a foreign and security policy have occurred in response to external pressures, usually involving Russia or other parts of Eastern Europe, combined with the internal dynamics of relations between its major member states. The establishment of the European security and defence policy (ESDP) during the last two years has been no exception.

The external pressures have come from the West Balkans, where the Union's inability to secure its interest in a stable peace without the predominant role of the United States has been only too apparent. With uncertainty as to how far the Americans will accept any necessary future involvement, the case for strengthening the Union's capacity in the field of defence has gained support. In addition, the British government's desire to be at the centre of EU affairs, while not yet participating in the euro, gave it a motive for playing a leading part in another major field. So Britain decided to initiate, together with France, the establishment of a European defence capacity.

In December 1998, President Chirac and Prime Ministers Blair and Jospin accordingly issued the St Malo declaration proposing structures and a capacity for autonomous European action in the field of defence. The project was taken further at the European Council meeting in Köln in June 1999, which also adopted the Common Strategy on Russia. It was agreed that the Union should put into effect the European security and defence policy, with a capacity to undertake tasks connected with peacekeeping. The European Council in Helsinki in December then took the decision to establish a rapid reaction force some 60 thousand strong, comprising contingents from those states willing to be involved, that could be deployed within sixty days and remain in position for at least a year. The force was to undertake 'Petersberg tasks' (named after the place near Bonn where they had earlier been defined), which included humanitarian and rescue operations, as well as peace-keeping and crisis management including 'the use of combat forces in peace-making.'[132] Defence ministers join the foreign ministers' Council when defence is on the agenda; and there is a Political and Security Committee at ambassadorial level, together with a Military Committee of member states' defence chiefs assisted by a Military Staff. At the Nice European Council in December 2000, a long list of nuts and bolts to firm up the arrangements was agreed.[133]

A lot has been done since December 1998 towards providing the Union with a usable military capacity. Problems remain, including differences between Britain and France about the relationship with Nato, and the question of using Nato facilities such as transport aircraft, satellite intelligence and planning facilities requiring unanimous agreement of the Nato members that is in the process of being obtained from Turkey. But the project has already attracted considerable interest from Russia, and in particular the possibility of participating when the EU undertakes Petersberg tasks. In the new situation following the terrorist attacks of September 2001, it may not be long before such opportunities arise. Russia has likewise welcomed the decision of the EU-Russia Summit in October 2001 to hold monthly meetings between the EU Political and Security Committee 'Troika' and Russian representatives.[134] If the ESDP proceeds as planned, it will add another significant strand to the Union's policy of forging a partnership with Russia, which is outlined in its Common Strategy.

The Common Strategy on Russia

A key to the successful launching of a policy in the Union is a combination of a general interest of the member states, which are therefore prepared to accept it, with the particular interest of a major member state that is ready to promote it. In the case of the Common Strategy on Russia, its significance for European security is generally appreciated, while Germany is particularly committed. Geography and history have made Germans acutely aware of the need for stable and constructive relations with their neighbours to the East, on grounds of both security and prosperity, so they have promoted the Union's policies for both enlargement to Central and Eastern Europe and partnership with Russia. History and geography have also brought home to Germans the benefits of union with their neighbours to the West, so they have also pressed for deepening the EU by strengthening its federal elements: hence their desire to 'communitise' the common foreign and security policy. Thus the German Presidency in the first half of 1999 not only helped to carry forward the ESDP but also worked hard to secure adoption of the Common Strategy on Russia at the European Council at Köln in June - only one month after the Amsterdam Treaty, with its provision for common strategies, entered into force.

The Common Strategy, which applies until June 2003 in the first instance, combines aims of a kind that has gained ground in foreign policy in recent years, seeking to encourage the development of a market economy and pluralist democracy, with the more traditional aims regarding security and economic relations.[135] The aims of the newer type are to favour 'a stable, open and pluralistic democracy in Russia, governed by the rule of law and underpinning a prosperous market economy'. This, as Solana put it in his Stockholm speech, should help Russia and the EU 'to live in harmony together.'[136] Aims of the more traditional type envisage 'intensified co-operation with Russia' for 'maintaining European stability, promoting global security and responding to the common challenges of the continent.'

The Common Strategy presented a compendium of what are for the most part the Union's existing relevant policies. For helping to consolidate 'democracy, the rule of law and public institutions in Russia', Tacis has, as chapter one showed, been the Union's principal instrument; and the Strategy stressed activities such as training programmes, exchanges, a wide range of twinning programmes, scholarships and other contacts. For supporting 'civic society', which is an essential foundation for pluralist democracy, the Strategy also mentioned similar activities, and for supporting 'the process of economic reform' a range of the policies examined in chapter one. In addition to these activities, the Strategy included the idea of a 'high-level policy dialogue' to promote the development of the market economy. Experience warns that this would be worse than useless unless the participants from the side of the Union have a deep enough understanding of the problems of the Russian economy. But the EU-Russia Summit of October 2001 may have placed the proposal on a firmer footing when it decided, as we saw in chapter one, to set up a joint High-Level Group to consider opportunities for 'greater integration and legislative co-operation', including an energy partnership, as bases for a Common European Economic Area.[137]

Much of the activity to 'support the integration of Russia into a wider area of co-operation in Europe', as the Common Strategy put it, was also considered in chapter one; and the Strategy mentioned in particular programmes to train Russian managers and entrepreneurs; the direct interest of the EU in areas of Russian expertise such as science, aerospace and energy;

and the free trade area project, with the cautious policy of examining 'how to create the necessary conditions' for its future establishment. The Strategy also included co-operation on nuclear safety; environmental protection; trans-European networks (TENs) in the field of transport; and energy, including the Energy Charter Treaty which aims among other things to increase the confidence of potential investors in Russian energy projects and whose ratification Russia had not yet, at the time of writing, completed. Co-operation was mentioned in fields such as health, welfare and culture. The Union also expressed particular interest in the fight against crime, money laundering, traffic in drugs and human beings and in police and judicial co-operation. Fighting against terrorism was, remarkably, omitted from that list, though it has since been mentioned in EU-Russia summit meetings and in particular, following the terrorist attacks of 11 September, in the meeting of 3 October 2001.

As regards 'stability and security in Europe and beyond', the call for 'intensified co-operation' in the Common Strategy document doubtless reflected disappointment with the results of the PCA's work in this field so far. The Union is to 'consider ways to give more continuity [...] to the existing political dialogue'. One such way could be for the Union itself to be less apt to break off the dialogue when it disapproves of something that Russia has done. The idea of facilitating Russian participation in the Union's Petersberg missions is also included, as is that of 'promoting arms control and the implementation of existing agreements', which presents the Union with an interesting problem in relation to the current American missile defence policy.

It is too early to judge the impact of this first example of a Common Strategy on what the Union is actually doing. The Declaration on majority voting does not seem to have had much effect on the behaviour of the member states which adopted it and hence on the effectiveness of this new departure in the CFSP. The Strategy's stipulation that each incoming Presidency is to present to the Council a work plan to implement the strategy could do no harm if the Presidency were to accept, at least for the most part, the proposals of the High Representative and the Commissioner for external relations. But if each state tries to put its own stamp on the strategy, the weakness to which

Holbrook referred can only be accentuated. Another institutional anomaly is the failure to mention the directly elected European Parliament, despite the facts that democracy is one of the strategy's major themes, the PCA has established a Parliamentary Co-operation Committee and the Russians themselves were soon, in their reciprocal Medium-term Strategy, to propose co-operation between the European and the Russian Parliaments. Perhaps the most damaging weakness of all was, however, the consensus that no new resources are to be allocated to support the strategy. Southern member states in particular have held that Russia and the Central and East European countries already account for too large a share of the Union's resources.[138] The first words of the Common Strategy affirm that 'a stable, democratic and prosperous Russia, firmly anchored in a united Europe free of new dividing lines, is essential to lasting peace on the continent.' A consensus that the Union's contribution to this will entail no additional cost does not make sense.

Russia's Medium-term Strategy for relations with the EU

Four months after the European Council adopted the Common Strategy on Russia, Vladimir Putin, who was then Prime Minister, delivered Russia's response at the EU-Russia Summit in Helsinki in October 1999. This was a 'Medium-term Strategy for Development of Relations between the Russian Federation and the European Union (2000-2010).'[139] A British observer found it 'a demanding and irritable response', which resented 'what it felt to be a tone of condescension and hubris' in the Union's Common Strategy.[140] But it nevertheless covered an agenda similar to that of the Union and declared the aim of 'laying the foundation for advanced partnership relations between the Russian Federation and the European Union in the future.'

Evidently appreciative of Tacis, Russia pressed for increased scope of the Union's programmes of technical and other assistance. It wanted continued EU help in seeking accession to the WTO but went beyond the Common Strategy in calling for discussions to consider 'the availability of conditions for the establishment of a free trade area'. Its interest in participation of Russian regions in developing the partnership corresponded to the policies of Tacis and the EBRD.

Whereas the Union's Common Strategy had mentioned the euro only in passing, the Medium-term Strategy stressed the potential for its use by Russia and Russian enterprises. While a close relationship with the currency of Russia's principal trading partner makes good economic sense, it also accords with Russia's policy of countering American global hegemony, which has likewise been a motive for Russian enthusiasm for the development of the Union's ESDP and defence capacity. The Medium-term Strategy, responding to the Common Strategy, looked forward to promoting practical co-operation with WEU and the Union in matters such as 'crisis settlement' and peace-making operations. It was also explicit about its aim to counterbalance 'the Nato-centrism' in Europe and 'ensure pan-European security by the Europeans themselves', though adding that this should be 'without isolation' of the US and Nato. While, as the Common Strategy made clear, co-operation with Russia in the field of security is in the Union's interests, Russians have been left in no doubt that partnership with Russia complements, not replaces, the Union's partnership with the United States. Since the Medium-term Strategy was issued, the tendency in Moscow has indeed been to accept that the European members of Nato remain firmly bound to the Atlantic Alliance; and the improvement of relations between Russia and the US following the terrorist attacks on New York and Washington should ease the trilateral relationship between them and the Union. In this perspective, the evidence that a large part of the Russian elite gives the EU precedence over all other partnerships can only be warmly welcomed by the Union.[141]

The path to partnership did not run smoothly

The Union's reaction to the first war in Chechnya, in delaying the entry into force of the Partnership and Co-operation Agreement until December 1997, three and a half years after it had been signed, lost valuable time for developing the political dialogue, even if the trade provisions were for the most part applied. When, in August 1999, Chechen rebels attacked the neighbouring Republic of Dagestan, also like Chechnya a part of the Russian Federation, the Union at first expressed its sympathy with Russia but, when the Russian offensive was launched in October, the Union's disapproval again pervaded the relationship. At the EU-Russia Summit in Helsinki on 22 October, when

Putin handed over the Russian Medium-term Strategy, Chechnya dominated the discussions;[142] and thus began another period of lost chances, though this time a shorter one. The European Council's declaration on the subject at its meeting in Helsinki in December not only condemned the bombardment of Chechen cities but also called for a review of the Common Strategy.

The succeeding Portuguese Presidency produced a late and very limited work plan for the strategy; some provisions of the PCA were again suspended; and some Tacis funds were switched to humanitarian assistance. On 24 January 2000 the General Affairs Council decided on sanctions against Russia: suspension of the signature of an agreement on co-operation in science and technology; suspension of preferences and a toughening of anti-dumping policy on imports from Russia; and refocusing the Tacis programme on democracy and networks in civil society as well as humanitarian assistance. While the latter was doubtless no bad thing in itself, the consequence was a reduction of Tacis allocations for the Russian programme from €140 million in 1998 to less than €100 million in 1999 and 2000.

Plain-speaking condemnation of Russia's methods of dealing with the Chechen problem would be a legitimate reaction, though the Union's recriminations were hardly timed appropriately only a few months after the end of the bombing campaign against Serbia. Some practical measures may also have been justified. But crowding out the dialogue on the longer-term relationship and imposing a wide range of sanctions, even if designed so as to avoid too much disruption to existing programmes, was a misjudgement of the requirements for building a long-term relationship.

This was before long recognised by political leaders in member states. In March 2000 Tony Blair visited Moscow, followed in June, shortly after Vladimir Putin had been installed as President, by Gerhard Schröder. In May, the EU-Russia Summit had already been held in Moscow in an atmosphere of goodwill; and by June the European Council in Feira affirmed that 'a strong and healthy partnership must be maintained between the EU and Russia'.

While the return to normal relations with Russia after only half a year showed good sense, it was also an implicit admission that the scope of the

Union's initial reaction had been ill judged. It has been suggested that policy was driven too much by the reactions of media;[143] and most of the media do not give weight to the longer-term needs of the relationship with Russia. The fundamental error was to suppose that increased respect for human rights in Russia depends more on international opinion than on the development of a law-based democracy; and that is more likely to be influenced by a steady development of the Tacis programme, with its contribution to a wide range of mutual contacts and to the transition to a society and economy subject to the rule of law, than by condemnatory declarations. It has been justly observed that 'human rights in Russia are far better protected than before, although, not surprisingly, things are not perfect'.[144] It is unwise to interrupt activities that help to consolidate this improvement, as well as the building of the relationship between Russia and the Union.

The West Balkans

The EU's condemnation of Russia over Chechnya and interruption of the development of the Common Strategy followed only four months after the end of the bombing campaign against Yugoslavia that began in March 1999 and ended in June with the visit to Belgrade of Martti Ahtisaari and Viktor Chernomyrdin. That war did eventually result in the overthrow of the Milosevic regime, which the Serbian voters finally accomplished in 2001. But the so-called 'zero deaths strategy' by which it was conducted was highly questionable, killing some five hundred civilians and destroying much of the Serbian economy. Tony Blair had argued that Nato should also prepare for a ground war in order not to be totally dependent on that strategy, but most other Nato powers did not support him. As that embodiment of neo-realism, Henry Kissinger, put it: 'A strategy that vindicates its moral convictions only from an altitude above 15,000 feet, and in the process devastates Serbia and makes Kosovo unliveable, has already produced more refugees and casualties than any conceivable alternative mix of force and diplomacy would have. It deserves to be questioned on both political and moral grounds.'[145]

Kissinger also pointed out that relations with Russia had been undermined. Support for the transition to democracy and the market economy was weakened; and Russians who were inclined to doubt the political wisdom and morality of the Chechen war could be forgiven for regarding the EU condemnation as hypocritical. A significant element in Russians' attitudes to the two wars was their adherence to the distinction between action within a sovereign state and an attack on another one. While western democracies, with their experience of half a century of mutual co-operation and integration, have increasingly come to see intervention in the affairs of another state as a normal aspect of democratic life, Russians have lacked that experience. It has indeed been pointed out that many of Russia's failings could have occurred in western countries not so long ago.[146] While not turning a blind eye to such failings, those who have experienced the past half-century in western democracies should not forget the distance that Russia has, in the past few years, travelled from the former Soviet system.

The war over Kosovo demonstrated how the EU's policies towards Central and East European countries may affect its relations with Russia and even Russians' attitudes towards the process of economic and political transition; and there is a positive as well as a negative side of this coin. The co-operation with Russian contingents in Bosnia and Kosovo has been satisfactory for both sides; and the effect of the Union's role in reconstruction and civilian peace-keeping in the West Balkans should be positive, particularly if the results of its efforts in Serbia are demonstrably beneficial.

The Union has, indeed, an opportunity in the West Balkans to develop its capacity as the world's leading power in the field of soft security. Its annual budgetary allocation of around a billion euros for assistance in the region over the seven years 2000-06, of which two-fifths is to go to democratic Serbia, is not over-generous, when economic reconstruction and building the market economies are added to tasks such as clearing mines, counter-terrorism, monitoring elections, deploying and training police and help for institution-building. But the EU is by far the largest contributor to support the creation of conditions for stability and prosperity in the region. Patten has proposed that the capacity to undertake the most urgent of such activities be combined in a 'non-military rapid reaction facility'. While most of the elements of such a capacity already exist, the ability to put them on the ground with the necessary human and financial resources quickly enough can be crucial. Success with such urgent action as well as with longer-term programmes of support would be much more satisfactory than military intervention after fighting has begun, and at only a fraction of the cost. As a framework for stabilisation in the region, the EU has initiated the Stability Pact for South-East Europe. It has also concluded Stability and Association Agreements with the several West Balkan states, the titles of which imply that, like the other Central and East Europeans, they too may expect eventually to qualify for membership of the Union.

The promotion of stability in the West Balkans is a very difficult task and success is by no means assured. But progress towards it, particularly in relation to Serbia, would make a positive contribution to the Union's relations with Russia. It has been suggested that, if sufficient progress is made and if mutual confidence between the EU and Russia grows sufficiently, it might be possible to envisage a stability pact for the South Caucasus, with the participation of the Union as well as Russia, Armenia, Azerbaijan and Georgia, which could become an 'outstanding example of preventative conflict diplomacy.'[147] But the conditions for that to become possible are doubtless some way down the road.

Enlargement

While opposing further enlargement of Nato, Russian officials have come to regard EU enlargement as good for Russia; and this has been encouraged by President Putin.[148] But many aspects of the accession of Central and East European states could be awkward for Russia and the Union needs to take them seriously if damage is not to be done to the prospects for partnership.

While the Central and East Europeans have already shifted in the direction of the Union the bulk of their trade, it remains important for Russia. Although, as Shishkov shows in chapter three, their tariffs on most items will be reduced when they join, problems will arise, particularly in the field of agriculture and more generally with the switch to the Union's harmonised standards and regulations. Foreign investment is already being attracted to these countries in anticipation of their membership and this will doubtless intensify as they accede, which may divert some investment that could have gone to Russia; but there will also be investments in Russia from at least some of them. There could be difficulties about agreement on the construction of trans-European transport networks, particularly pipelines, between Russia and the Union, though there is less likely to be trouble from countries that expect to join the Union before long than from those that do not. In general, Shishkov observes, the Russians have found the Commission helpful in seeking solutions for potential problems; and it is to be hoped that the same will apply to member states.

Many sensitivities relate to frontiers; and the Russian Medium-term Strategy aims at 'the construction of a united Europe without dividing lines.' The EU's external frontier is inevitably a line that divides its economy, where Union law prevails, from neighbouring economies where it does not; and the same applies to the Schengen arrangements for control of people crossing frontiers. But it is understandable and proper that Russians should wish to minimise any consequent inconveniences.

With the accession of Estonia and Latvia, the Union will share frontiers with Russia that were formerly inside the Soviet Union and will bring substantial Russian-speaking populations within the Union. As Kaliningrad's borders are with Poland and Lithuania, its inhabitants' access by land to the rest of the Russian Federation will be either through Lithuania and Latvia, or through Lithuania and Belarus or Poland and Belarus. The EU being generally well viewed by Russians, it is hoped that enlargement will ensure a good standard of behaviour in the new member states in such matters as frontier controls. But it is also feared that technical complications could exacerbate Russians' tendency to feel excluded, with knock-on political effects.[149] The Phare programme has helped Central and East European countries to develop their capacity to deal with problems of frontier control towards a level of performance that is a condition of accession; and the Union needs to regard the ability to provide an efficient service for bona fide travellers as an essential criterion alongside the ability to keep undesirable people out. It has been proposed that the Union ensure that multi-entry visas be issued free of charge to residents of the border regions and that adequate consular services be provided.[150] Co-operation between border control forces and law enforcement agencies on both sides of the frontier also strengthens mutual confidence.[151]

With a view to the longer term, the European Parliament has proposed the establishment of an EU border control force, to share the burden among the member states and ensure effectiveness.[152]

There are other political sensitivities regarding relations between Russia and states that are negotiating accession, arising out of history and the Soviet experience in particular. There are Russian fears that some of them could hinder the development of the relationship between the EU and Russia and even stir up anti-Russian sentiment in the Union. The EU's influence in persuading Estonia and Latvia to improve the lot of their large Russian-speaking minorities has been appreciated; and it is in the interest of the Union that this be maintained, as one and a half million contented Russian-speakers among its citizens would be a positive, rather than a negative, factor in relations with Russia. More broadly, it is an important diplomatic task for the EU to ensure that the candidates, both before and after their accession, contribute to building the partnership with Russia. As well as resentments that they may harbour, which the EU should seek to mitigate, they share between them a store of knowledge of Russia which should be of considerable value to this end.

For Russia, the enlargement of Nato is another matter. One way of putting it is that Nato has up to now been seen by the Russian security elite as an instrument of American foreign policy which could revert to Cold War attitudes, and that whereas Nato's enlargement to Central Europe has been regarded as a threat to Russian national interests, enlargement to the Baltic states would be seen as a threat to Russian national security.[153] Given the legacy of history, it is understandable that the Baltic States want to obtain the maximum possible guarantees of security. But their membership of the Union will be a powerful deterrent to any misuse of Russian power against them, which would put the whole of Russia's relations with the Union at risk. The Union might well conclude that, given the extension of Nato membership in Central Europe, the development of stable relations with Russia, together with Nato's existing membership, is the best safeguard for the security of Baltic States. In the new situation following the terrorist attack on the US, however, a change in the relationship between Russia and Nato seems possible. Suggestions have included a special treaty between Russia and Nato, a form of associate membership, or eventually full membership. In such a context, mutually agreed solutions to the problem of Nato enlargement to the Baltic States might well be found.

Kaliningrad

It would not be surprising if Russia were to react nervously to the prospect that one of its Oblasts will be surrounded by the Union. But the present policy, as confirmed in Russia's Medium-term Strategy, is to suggest that Kaliningrad should become a 'pilot region' for EU-Russia co-operation; and the Commission's policy papers on enlargement and Kaliningrad have been seen as co-operative.[154] There are, however, some difficult problems to resolve. Although the garrison has been reduced from 100,000 in the Soviet period to 30,000, the question of military transport is still a worry, as are power supplies and economic development. There is anxiety because the existing arrangements for visa-free crossing to Poland and Lithuania will be terminated; and a local official has observed unease in Moscow that there could be a growing tendency towards separatism.[155]

The regime for border-crossing is important for people in Kaliningrad, many of whom want to visit Poland or Lithuania, some quite frequently. Even though many travellers have to wait hours to cross, the ability to do so without a visa is much appreciated.[156] But the Finns, for whom control of their border with Russia is very important, will insist on a regime on a par with their own;[157] and proper passports will be required. It has been pointed out that this will be very difficult for local people unless member states open consulates in Kaliningrad, which Sweden and Latvia have taken steps to do; and it has been suggested that some of them could share the costs.[158] Low-cost or free multiple-entry visas are indicated, which Estonia, while requiring passports, is ready to issue to locals without a fee.[159] While these are minor details compared with the great issues involved in EU-Russia relations, they could, if care is not taken to get them right, cause disproportionate aggravation - or, if well handled, goodwill. The Commission's quick response in allocating €2 million to improvement of border crossing between Lithuania and Kaliningrad was described by a Russian observer as 'quite inspiring.'[160]

Transit to and from the rest of Russia, with the crossing of at least three borders, is more problematic, and military transport yet more so. The Union's arrangements for co-operation on police and judicial affairs will, moreover, have to cope with a wide range of cross-border criminal activity, which will be a test of the EU-Russia collaboration that the strategies of both sides envisage in that field.

The widening gap between the economic levels of Kaliningrad and its faster-growing neighbours is a cause of concern. Tacis has sought to address this with €15 million of assistance in the 1990s; and Patten has promised a further €15 million to promote development and suggested that an EU representative office could be opened there.[161] Given Kaliningrad's special situation, the idea has been mooted that the EU institutes a special fund to which states with a particular interest in the Oblast's development would contribute.[162] The importance of harmonising Kaliningrad with the EU's economic space has been underlined, including assistance for local enterprises to adopt EU standards.[163]

Patten sees regional integration with Kaliningrad's neighbours as an 'engine of growth'.[164] Moves in that direction have, however, so far been limited. Transport links are crucial. But the main trans-European links between Russia and the Union will by-pass Kaliningrad, though connecting spurs are being studied. There is inter-regional co-operation with neighbouring Polish voivodships and with Schleswig-Holstein, but they have not so far made an important contribution. Proposals that the remit of the Union's structural funds be extended to promote cross-border regions could be particularly relevant.[165] With an effective development programme, Kaliningrad could become the pilot region for co-operation envisaged by Putin; and the EU's Northern Dimension, involving the neighbouring states around the Baltic, is well placed to help it to do so.[166]

The Northern Dimension

The Northern Dimension project was launched by Finland in 1997. With a thousand kilometres of shared border, the Finns are acutely conscious of their relationship with Russia; and while worry about threats to security has changed its nature since the Soviet Union disintegrated, there are new concerns about such matters as crime, illegal migration and the environment.

Whereas in the West Balkans the EU has been drawn into issues of hard security, Finland has focused its initiative on soft security, fearing that elements of traditional security policy could impede the development of practical co-operation.[167] Prime Minister Lipponen defined 'the basic aim' as being to 'integrate Russia into Europe as a democracy and a market economy.'[168]

With primary emphasis on sustainable development, the main fields envisaged for co-operation were natural resources, environment, transport and energy infrastructures, and border management, together with an array of specifics from research to health, employment services and culture. The participants were the Scandinavians; Estonia, Latvia, Lithuania and Poland as candidates for EU membership; and Russia, with particular reference to its North-West and Kaliningrad. The intention was to promote co-operation among them and to increase the EU's awareness of Northern concerns.

The European Council in December 1997 accepted the idea of the Northern Dimension at the same time as the Partnership and Co-operation Agreement entered into force. But, along with the PCA, its progress was hampered by the Russian financial crisis of 1998 and the outbreak of the second Chechen war in 1999. Nor was this all that made it hard to retain the attention of member states. There was also the absence of any big state among the Northern Dimension's sponsors, the fear of Southern states that it would distract attention from their concerns, and the lack of its own instruments, in particular an EU budget line.

Several developments have made member states more receptive since 1999: the approach of accession by Poland and the Baltic states; the Kaliningrad problem linked with it; greater awareness of the need for oil and gas from North-West Russia; President Putin's favourable attitude to relations with the Union; and the Common Strategy as a comprehensive framework for the Union's Russian policy. So the European Council in June 2000 was able to adopt the Commission's Action Plan for the Northern Dimension, setting out policies for the years 2000-03.[169]

The aims were defined as security, stability, sustainable development and democracy. Among the fields of activity listed, energy and transport infrastructure were particularly significant, given the Union's need for oil and gas from North-West Russia. The environment and nuclear safety reflected concern over the fact that one-fifth of the world's nuclear reactors are in that region, some of them in bad shape, in addition to huge deposits of nuclear waste without adequate processing and storage facilities. Fields such as education, health and social administration were mentioned; and there was greater emphasis on cross-border questions such as the fight against crime. There was again special mention of Kaliningrad.

Not surprisingly in a Commission policy paper, the Action Plan was a framework for the co-ordination of existing policies and programmes of the Union and the states; and the European Council asked the Commission to take the lead in its implementation. All this had the merit of inserting the Northern Dimension in the Union's mainstream. But a Finnish view was that it suffered from being compartmentalised between the Union's pillars and the Commission's Directorates General; it remained limited by existing budget lines, in programmes such as Phare, Tacis and INTERREG, without extra finance; and it lacked a concept or new impulses that could give added value to what the Union was doing already.[170]

While it may be hoped that the process of reforming the Commission will lead to better co-ordination among the Directorates General, the Union's division into separate pillars is a weakness at the heart of the CFSP which can be rectified only by treaty reform. Meanwhile, we have to make do with the treaties as they stand. But greater financial resources could add impetus to the Northern Dimension, as to other elements of the Union's policy towards Russia. New impulses might also come from the approaching enlargement, as Poland and the Baltic states begin to play their part in the Union's affairs.

The proposal that Kaliningrad become a pilot region for co-operation could provide a stimulus. So also could a special effort to strengthen the Union's relationship with North-West Russia. This would build on the priority given to Novgorod by Tacis and the EBRD and to St Petersburg by the latter. It would respond to the suggestion in Russia's Medium-term Strategy that its regions play a part in developing the partnership with the Union and might be appreciated by President Putin, given his background in St Petersburg. It would also serve two of the Union's important interests, in a stable source of energy supplies and environmental security.

Climate change

There is growing evidence that global warming is one of the gravest threats to the security of mankind in this century. The EU, with the strength of the green interest in its politics, is the leading force for action to deal with it; and partnership with Russia could be a key to its success.

The Community had already played an important part in the international agreement of 1987 to control emissions of chlorofluorocarbons (CFCs) that could destroy the ozone layer and thus endanger life on earth; and a decade later it was central to the negotiation of the Kyoto Protocol to stem the emissions of CO_2 and other greenhouse gases that threaten to lead to a very dangerous degree of global warming. The consensus of the International Panel on Climate Change (IPCC), comprising a hundred and fifty of the world's leading scientific experts on the subject, is that if the emissions are not controlled, global temperatures will rise by between 1.4 per cent and 5.8 per cent during the twenty first century.[171] The consequent rise in sea level would not only submerge some small islands but also endanger low-lying coastal areas throughout the world; lead to violent storms, floods and other disasters; and cause desertification such as to cut food production in many countries, for example in India by as much as one-fifth. The EU would suffer disasters too, though on a less horrendous scale than in some other parts of the world; but Europe would be affected by instability elsewhere, including pressures of mass migration and military security risks.[172]

The EU and member states take such a prospect seriously and it has been suggested that the Union will, given its economic and political weight, be the most important global player in the future.[173] It proposed at Kyoto that the total of industrialised countries' emissions of CO_2 be cut by 2010 to a level 15 per cent below that of 1990. But the US wanted merely to stabilise CO_2 and other, less important greenhouse gases at the 1990 level; and the outcome was agreement on a cut of CO_2 by 8 percent for the Union, 7 per cent for the US and 5.2 per cent for the group of industrialised countries as a whole by the period 2008-2012. This was still far short of the reduction of 60 per cent or more that is estimated by Sir John Houghton, chairman of the IPCC, to be necessary in less than a hundred years, but nevertheless a significant step towards it.[174] A report by government experts together with representatives of industry and environmental groups, set up by the Commission, has estimated that cost-effective measures could cut emissions in the Union by twice the Kyoto target for an extra outlay of €3.7 billion a year; and the Royal Commission on Environmental Polution called for a cut of 60 per cent in carbon emissions by 2050.[175]

The need for the Union to confirm its role as the most important player was not long in coming, when the new Bush Administration cancelled US participation in the Kyoto Protocol, partly because, with emissions already 13 per cent higher than in 1990, the reduction of 7 per cent from that level was becoming very difficult to achieve, but also in reaction against commitments under multilateral agreements. But the Union managed at the Conference of the Parties in Bonn and Marrakech in the second half of 2001 to secure commitment to ratify the Protocol from enough states to enable it to come into force, with average cuts that are significant even if less than envisaged at Kyoto. The agreement of states accounting for at least 55 per cent of the industrial countries' 1990 emissions was required; and without participation of the US, whose share had been 36.2 per cent, it was essential to secure the agreement of Russia, with 17.4 per cent, and Japan, with 8.5 per cent, to add to the Union's share of 24.2 per cent and those of the states negotiating accession. Given the huge American share, it is necessary to seek to bring the US on board as much as possible and as soon as possible. But it has been demonstrated that partnership with Russia is a crucial element in the Union's strategy for building global security in this field.

Because of the enormously wasteful consumption of energy in the Soviet system, together with the subsequent fall in output, Russian emissions of greenhouse gases are already as much as 30 per cent below the level of 1990. So Russia can benefit significantly from the 'flexible mechanisms' that were devised to secure American agreement to the Kyoto Protocol, enabling countries to enlarge their emission quotas by buying rights from countries that were not using theirs in full. Russia benefits, too, from the rights acquired through the possession of carbon sinks, mainly forests, which absorb carbon emissions. A further mechanism, which is proving useful for both Russia and the EU, is 'joint implementation', comprising projects whereby one industrial country can 'buy' emission rights by helping another to improve its use of energy. An example is the use of software developed by Ruhrgas to improve the energy efficiency of Gazprom's distribution network, with Gazprom deriving profit from the cost savings, in which the German company can share as well as becoming entitled to emission rights.[176]

The Union was reluctant to accept the American demand for such mechanisms, on the grounds that all states should make a full substantive contribution to the reduction of emissions. It has also been pointed out that it is the countries which are industrially more advanced that are capable of developing the technologies for freeing economies from their dependence on fossil fuels; and the flexible mechanisms weaken their incentive to do so.[177] But meanwhile, those mechanisms are financially advantageous for Russia, and the more so to the extent that the US, with a strong propensity to buy emission rights, participates, and that Russia improves its own energy efficiency.

Members of the Russian delegation at the earlier session of the Conference of the Parties at The Hague in December 2000 were willing to discuss ways of ensuring that the money obtained by emissions trading would be used for 'environmentally legitimate' purposes and the head of the delegation said that Russia would be ready to consider using such funds 'for further reduction of greenhouse gas emissions.'[178] With Russia's consumption of energy per unit of production several times greater than in the Union, this would contribute substantially to the control of global warming. But it would not be easy to achieve, given the pressures on the Russian budget from a number of powerful interests. So the Union may be well-advised to seek a formal agreement on it with the Russian government, which could be linked with an allocation for similar purposes from Tacis, together with plans for investments from the EBRD and the European Investment Bank.

Not least among the potential Russian contributions would be the use of its scientific talent to develop technologies for producing relevant equipment. This could be an element in the conversion of redundant capacity in the defence industries, towards which projects of 'joint implementation' with companies from the EU could help.

Co-operation in this field could become an important element in the developing EU-Russia partnership, responding to a major interest of the Union, and where Russia has much to contribute and much to gain. Russia would also share the Union's interest in the maximum possible US participation because it would strengthen the market for emission rights. But while the Union has significant achievements to its credit in relation to the Kyoto Protocol, its institutions remain seriously defective. 'It spends so much time negotiating with itself', as expert observers have put it, that little time remains for negotiating with other countries.[179] In negotiating on trade, the Union is more effective, with its exclusive competence in the framework of the European Community and with the Commission as its negotiator; and the same applied for the Montreal Protocol on control of CFCs. For global warming, however, where the ramifications reach into a range of member states' energy policies, there are mixed competences of both the Union and the states. Thus the negotiations are led by the Council's President-in-Office, with all the inconveniences of a change of negotiator every six months, and unanimity is required for all that concerns the states' competences. Although the Union played an essential part in the conferences at Kyoto, Bonn and Marrakech more effective arrangements will be needed if it is to cope with the challenges it will confront as global leader in this field in the future: as a 'driver of policies', it has been suggested, for a decent life for humanity in the centuries to come.[180] It will, among other things, have to ensure that much deeper cuts are agreed before too long; that the US participates in them sufficiently; that Third World countries are brought in on a basis they can regard as equitable; that the IPCC institutions are strengthened, with the aim of establishing an effective rule of law;[181] and that partnership with Russia is effective.

Russia, the EU and the US

Among Russian conservatives, in the sense of those wishing to conserve elements of Soviet thinking, 'multipolarism' signified a struggle against global American hegemony, including the objective of separating the EU from the US. But early in the year 2000, foreign minister Igor Ivanov expressed the view that a multipolar system should be seen, not as an anti-American policy, but rather as a 'foundation of the building of the future world order'.[182]

The United States itself has combined unilateralist proclivities with support for multilateral institutions.[183] But the Bush Administration, with its unilateralist stance on the Anti-Ballistic Missile Treaty and the Kyoto Protocol, as well as on agreements regarding hand guns, landmines and biological weapons, has appeared to be comfortable with the idea of a unipolar world. Its initial attitudes towards Russia were moreover typified by George W. Bush's remark, before assuming the Presidency, that he would try to end the flow of dollars to Russia, apart from programmes relating to disarmament; by defence secretary Donald Rumsfeld's 'casual disregard of Russia'; and by *The Economist*'s assessment of the Administration's view that 'Russia hardly matters'.[184] But exposure to the problems of government and the face-to-face encounter between Presidents Bush and Putin, together with the Republicans' loss of control of the Senate, soon began to moderate these gut reactions; and the events of 11 September 2001 may have induced a significant change in the Administration's outlook towards relationships with other countries and with Russia in particular. American policies towards both Russia and the strengthening of multilateral agreements and institutions are likely to remain different from those that prevail in the European Union. But there may well be a better prospect of US support for a constructive EU-Russia partnership.

Although, in the spectrum of European attitudes towards the US, Britain is the most inclined to comply with American policies, the view that this implies almost automatic acquiescence was contradicted by Tony Blair's vision of the Union as a potential 'superpower'.[185] As Chris Patten has pointed out, there are many areas of disagreement, including environmental policy and Americans' tendency to pursue extraterritorial powers combined with 'a neuralgic hostility to any external authority over their own affairs'.[186] A policy aiming to minimise the relationship between the EU and the US would however be entirely misconceived. Partnership between the world's two great centres of liberal democracy and market economy is clearly essential. But a unipolar view of the American place in the world is likewise misconceived.

Even as the only global superpower, the US cannot manage the world's affairs single-handed, without genuine partnerships and multilateral institutions. Nor will it remain the only superpower. China will, in the next decade or two, emerge as another, and probably the only other one, if the European Union fails to do so. A world dominated by those two superpowers, with their differing political concepts and interests, would be a dangerous place. It is a vital interest of the EU to foster partnership with the US, as far as possible on a basis of equality, at the same time as building partnerships with Russia and other major powers, and working to strengthen multilateral institutions. Even if the Bush Administration may still incline towards unilateralism and unipolarity, the EU should pursue a long-term policy designed to secure American co-operation in creating a multipolar system within a framework of effective multilateral institutions. But that policy can be sufficiently effective only in so far as the Union does in fact realise Blair's vision of itself becoming a superpower.

This prospect is not as remote as most people suppose. In the field of trade, where the EU has common instruments and Community-type institutions, it has long since been the equal of the US. Disputes attract the headlines. But from the Kennedy round of GATT negotiations in the 1960s to the establishment of the WTO in the 1990s, the Union and the US have worked to create a liberal trading system, with the Union latterly playing a leading role. The Union's own aid programme, at €7 billion a year, is the world's largest and, together with the member states, it provides over half of all international development assistance and two-thirds of all grant aid.[187] While the US and the dollar still dominate the global monetary system, the euro gives the Union instruments as potentially powerful in that field as it has with respect to trade. The British opt-out is a serious weakness and the institutions for external monetary policy are under-developed. But here too, given time and institutional reform, the Union can become the equal of the United States, while it has already achieved at least that status in the negotiations on climate change.

These are among the most important fields of international activity; and the Union has been developing a certain ability to use them together with policies that are more overtly in the field of soft security, as it has done in the West Balkans. But the institutions of the CFSP, based predominantly on intergovernmental unanimity, are not yet capable of deploying the Union's several instruments and policies in an external policy that could live up to Blair's vision.

As regards hard security, the Union is dwarfed by the American military capacity and will so remain at least for a long time to come. But the rapid reaction force should help to redress the balance where massive military force is not required; and the Union could, given reform of its institutions designed to make the CFSP effective, use its existing powers to become an equal partner of the US in all fields save that of defence. The alliance provides the Europeans with security against possible major threats. For the Americans, the EU's capacity in the field of soft security will reduce the risk of having to resort to hard security and may well prove of great value in the fight against terrorism. As Simon Huntington put it, moreover, 'The relationship with Europe is central to the success of American foreign policy. [...] Healthy co-operation with Europe is the prime antidote to the loneliness of American superpowerdom.'[188] It is also the only route whereby Americans can make the transition from sole superpower to a world in which power is effectively shared within multilateral institutions.

The EU, for its part, can best promote its interests in a stable and prosperous global system where it can do so in co-operation with the United States. But such a policy will not succeed without the participation of other major states. The Union needs to build partnerships with such states. The theme of this book is that Russia should, as Solana suggested, have priority among them.

Chapter 5:
EU-Russia Partnership as a Pillar for Building a Safe and Stable World System

John Pinder

The European Union's Common Strategy on Russia is of great potential importance. The Union's external economic relations still carry most weight, though other aspects of its common foreign policy, including security, are becoming increasingly significant. In order to play its full part in creating the partnership that is the declared aim of both the Union and Russia, the Union will have to combine both elements in a powerful and coherent policy much more effectively than it has done so far.

Economic relations

The Union's trade policy seeks to support Russian integration into the European and international economy. It has done much to open its own economy to imports from Russia, but should do more to liberalise its steel and agricultural sectors and to improve its anti-dumping procedures. The potential for higher imports of Russian gas and oil is particularly important for both the Union and Russia, but a secure framework for the massive investments must be assured. While Russia has appreciated the Union's help towards facilitating its membership of the World Trade Organisation, more thought will have to be given to creating the conditions, as the Partnership and Co-operation Agreement puts it, that will make an eventual free trade area with Russia feasible; and meanwhile to putting substance into the concept of the Common European Economic Area, which, given the potential of the Russian economy, should bring as much benefit to the EU as to Russia.

Foreign direct investment, with the accompanying transfer of management and technological skills, is a key to successful Russian economic development. But it waits on the establishment of a reliable rule of law, including proper corporate governance. The European Bank for Reconstruction and Development has been using its influence in this direction, which has also been a major objective of the Union's Tacis programme.

In line with the view that the basic requirement for Russian economic development is a dependable rule of law, with people in the public institutions and the economy who know how to make it work, the thrust of Tacis has been shifting towards emphasis on the legal, administrative and human infrastructure required for a successful market economy. Assistance to that end is a delicate operation that needs to be provided by people with a good understanding of Russian conditions. There are not many such in the Union and it should invest in the human resources required for this very important work.

Russia has expressed interest in various ways of using the euro that could be advantageous for the Union, which has, however, been slow to prepare a common external monetary policy that would enable it to respond, at least in part because its institutional arrangements are not adequate for the purpose. Nor has it made much progress towards forming a common policy in the international monetary institutions. Yet the influence of the United States on Russian macroeconomic policy and on the IMF has often been misconceived. Europeans, being closer to Russia and more aware of their interest in its success, should acquire at least as much influence in this field as the US.

The Union's economic policies towards Russia have on the whole been reasonably successful, in the very difficult conditions that Shishkov describes in chapter two. The end-of-decade report for the years 1991-2000 might be 'fairly satisfactory, but could do better'. More liberalisation is required where import restrictions remain. The importance of the euro should be reflected in the Union's external monetary policies towards Russia, including its influence in the international institutions. The EBRD should be given all the support it may need from member states and their representatives on its board, for its efforts to improve the conditions for direct foreign investment. Above all, Tacis should have the human and financial resources that it can usefully apply to its vital task of helping the Russians to establish the framework for a successful market economy. The thread that runs through all these ways of doing better is higher priority for the Union's Common Strategy on Russia and hence for its economic as well as other component parts.

Foreign and security policy

The Union's Common Strategy on Russia and Russia's Medium-term Strategy for its relations with the Union both addressed similar lists of fields for co-operation in building a long-term partnership.

One field that did not figure prominently, however, but is crucial for the future security of Europe and indeed the world as a whole, is common action against terrorism. Co-operation in this was proposed in the Russian strategy document but not in the Union's. The terrorist attack of 11 September 2001 has not only demonstrated that Russia was right and the Union wrong. It has also opened up the prospect of a new context for the EU-Russia partnership, with the EU giving it a higher priority owing to its evident significance for security, and greater American understanding and support; and this is reflected in the emphasis given to political and security co-operation in the Joint Statement of the EU-Russia Summit in October 2001.[189]

Another field, which was also not specified in the Common Strategy, but is probably yet more crucial for the future security of Europeans and of all mankind, is that of common action to counter global warming. Yet with the Union leading the international negotiations and Russia having an essential part to play, it should be a key element in the partnership.

Nor did the Common Strategy mention problems arising from the process of enlargement to Central and Eastern Europe, which influences relations between Russia and the Union in many ways. The candidate countries were, however, invited to associate themselves with actions under the Common Strategy; and the Union and its present member states should do what they can to persuade the Central and East European applicants to use their knowledge of Russia in ways that will help to smooth relations during the process of enlargement and to build the EU-Russia partnership. Given the will, they are well placed to make a constructive contribution to the relationship. For those that share borders with Russia, high standards of frontier controls are very important, as is the efficient and inexpensive provision of visas, while the other side of the coin is effective action against cross-border crime in co-operation with the authorities on the Russian side.

The question of frontier controls is particularly sensitive for inhabitants of Kaliningrad, many of whom need access to their immediate neighbours, Poland and Lithuania, and who can reach the rest of Russia overland only by passing in addition through either Latvia or Belarus. Since Poland and Lithuania are both future member states, the Union has a strong interest in Kaliningrad's social stability and economic health, in order that problems there will not spill over and damage the neighbourhood. So the Union should respond to Russia's suggestion that Kaliningrad become a pilot region for co-operation between them, through a special programme of assistance and promotion of investment aiming at its economic and social development.

The purpose of the Northern Dimension project is to foster a wide range of co-operation among states around the Baltic area, which include two present and four future member states as well as Russia, with special reference to its North-West region together with Kaliningrad. North-West Russia is of particular interest to the Union, as a potential source of large supplies of oil and gas as well as the location of nuclear power plants and waste that could cause acute environmental problems. There has, however, been some disappointment about the results of the Northern Dimension, due at least in part to the paucity of Union policy instruments, in particular budgetary resources, dedicated to putting substance into it. One reason for this is the reluctance of other member states, such as those of the Union's South, to see resources diverted from policies that interest them more. In line with the Union's time-honoured device of the package deal, it has been pointed out that the Northern and Southern dimensions of the CFSP need to be linked in order to avoid destructive rivalry between different regional groups of member states.[190]

While this principle can inhibit the Union's ability to choose priorities, the strategy towards Russia itself has a southern as well as a northern dimension, since Russia as well as the Union is interested in stability in the Balkans and, as Shishkov makes clear, has strong views about some of the actions, such as the war over Kosovo, in which states of the Union have been involved. The Union is the main source of help for reconstruction and the transition to democracy in the West Balkans and success in its endeavours should contribute to good relations with Russia. The Common Strategy on Russia indicates, moreover, that Russia could be invited to participate in peace-keeping operations initiated by the Union; and it was agreed, at the EU-Russia Summit of October 2001, to develop arrangements for such participation, as progress is made in the European Security and Defence Policy. The attitude of the Macedonian majority to Nato and EU efforts to help keep the peace in Macedonia at the time of writing indicates that Russian participation could indeed be valuable in such cases.

The development of the Union's new defence capacity might well have been a cause of contention with Russia. The positive Russian reaction is therefore encouraging. So also is the acceptance by the Russian government that the intention is to build a European pillar in Nato, not to undermine the alliance. But while the Union must not lose sight of the fact that the US will remain predominant in Nato at least for a long time to come, nor should it be deterred from building a more powerful defence capacity than is currently envisaged. American willingness to undertake operations that the Union regards as in its interest cannot be guaranteed, particularly when the US is absorbed in actions such as that against terrorists; and it is not rendered more likely by Europeans' military incapacity.

A growth of the Union's military capacity will involve a lengthy learning process, so any acceleration sudden enough to be disruptive is not feasible, even if it were desirable. A major transfer of competence for defence to the Union could, moreover, not be accomplished without solidly democratic and effective Union institutions to discharge the responsibility. While such institutions may be built in due course, the Union's policy in the field of security should meanwhile be to concentrate on making a success of the rapid reaction force and on further developing its already substantial capacity in the field of soft security: of action which promotes economic, social and political stability and is an essential complement to the ability to deploy armed force.

A major element in such a broad-based security policy must be the building of the partnership with Russia, which apart from its other benefits could, as Dmitri Trenin has put it, lead in the long run to 'embedding Russia in a Euro-Atlantic security community' or, in Lawrence Freedman's more explicit formulation, to Nato becoming 'a quite different institution - in effect, a pan-European security organisation', the logic of which process 'leads to the point where it can only be completed by including Russia.'[191]

The project of partnership will, however, not come to its due fruition unless it is seen in the context of a broader view of the part that the Union could play in the world and of a readiness to develop its structures in ways that will enable it to do what is necessary to play that part.

The Union's structure and the wider context

The Union's institutions are still not adequate to accomplish the tasks of establishing the partnership with Russia and the relationship that Europeans should have with the wider world. Richard Holbrook was right to say that 'Europe is better off institutionally today than it was at any time in the last century'; but his experience also justified his criticism that the Europeans need to 'clean up their procedures, make decisions more quickly, and come to terms with the basic issues of democracy and accountability'.[192]

Holbrook's experience was in the field of the Union's external relations, where the difficulties inherent in a union of fifteen states, most of them jealous of their sovereignty, is compounded by the division of responsibility between the Union's predominantly intergovernmental second pillar, in which decision-taking by unanimous agreement prevails, and the first, Community pillar where qualified majority voting normally applies in the Council and the Commission has a key role. This division is embodied in the roles of the CFSP's High Representative, Javier Solana, as the Secretary General of the Council, and Chris Patten as the Commissioner for external relations, who doubtless expressed the view of both of them when he said 'Luckily Javier Solana and I work extremely well together - but we are not much helped in that by the new institutional machinery'. It would, he went on to say, 'be absurd to divorce European foreign policy from the institutions which have been given responsibility for most of the instruments for its accomplishment: for external trade questions, including sanctions; for European external assistance; for many of the external aspects of Justice and Home Affairs'.[193] Yet the division between the Community pillar, which carries those responsibilities, and the CFSP pillar, while not going as far as divorce, is at least a form of separation. Member states have moreover focused on bilateral contacts rather than EU-Russia relations; and while there can be no doubting the importance of such contacts, particularly at the level of heads of member states' governments with President Putin, they should not be developed at the expense of the relationship between Russia and the Union as a whole.[194] Governments are not being realistic if they seek to form satisfactory partnerships with Russia separately, or to concentrate power exclusively in the Council, instead of recognising the potential of the Community system as the framework to work effectively towards the aims to which they committed themselves when they agreed on the Common Strategy.

The principle of subsidiarity indicates that sovereignty should be shared where the Union can be more effective than the member states acting separately; and it is not conceivable that Britain, or any other member state, could be seen, in Shishkov's words, as Russia's 'chief strategic partner.' Pooling sovereignty, 'when we choose to', as the Foreign Secretary has said, is the way to strengthen it.[195] The Union will not be able to match its words with deeds in building the partnership with Russia unless it makes that choice for the CFSP, moving towards majority voting and adequate competences for the Commission, together with sufficient budgetary support. Nor will such pooling of sovereignty be soundly based unless the Union's deficiency in democracy and accountability, to which Holbrook also drew attention, is rectified by strengthening the role of the European Parliament. The deliberations on reform starting with the European Council at Laeken in December 2001 offer an opportunity to make the Union more effective and democratic in such ways.

Nor is the Union's strategy on Russia likely to be sustained unless it forms part of a broader vision of the Union's external relations, which can unite the member states in a policy designed to promote security and stability in the wider world. An equal partnership with the United States, based on Union powers and institutions sufficient for that purpose in all fields other than defence, would be a basis for such a policy, with the Americans playing the predominant part in the field of hard security and the Europeans in that of soft security.

With that division of labour, a central task for the Union is the forging of the partnership with Russia, through common action in matters such as peace-keeping, climate change and the fight against terrorism and organised crime, together with a massive programme of assistance to help Russia complete its transformation into a mature market economy and pluralist democracy. It is a project for which the Union has a unique interest and potential capability. As Solana said in his Stockholm speech, development of the partnership with Russia is not only the most important, urgent and challenging task that the EU faces now, but even offers 'the greatest opportunity to affect the course of world affairs for the better and to begin the new century in a manner that will truly affect the course of world history.'[196] Rapid results should not be expected. But steady pursuit of the Union's Common Strategy, combined with reform to give the Union the necessary powers and institutions, offers the best chance of success in establishing a firm and fruitful partnership with Russia which could become a pillar for the building of a more stable and safer world.

notes

1 Javier Solana, 'The EU and Russia Strategic Partnership', speech delivered in Stockholm, 13 October 1999.

2 As suggested by Heinz Timmermann, *Russlands Strategie für die Europäische Union: Aktuelle Tendenzen, Konzeptionen und Perspektiven* (Köln: Bundesinstitut für ostwissenschaftliche und internationale Studien, 2000), p.9. He refers to an article by S. Markov, 'Manipulyativnaya demokratiya', *Nezavisimaya Gazeta*, 2 March 2000.

3 Jack Straw, Secretary of State for Foreign and Commonwealth Affairs, speech at The Royal Institute of International Affairs, 27 July 2001.

4 For more detail on the relationship up to 1991, see John Pinder, *The European Union and Eastern Europe* (London: Pinter Publishers for The Royal Institute of International Affairs, 1991).

5 'Agreement on Partnership and Co-operation, establishing a partnership between the European Communities and their Member States, of the one part, and the Russian Federation, of the other part', *Official Journal L 327*, pp.3-69.

6 David Gowan, *How the EU can help Russia* (London: Centre for European Reform, 2000), pp.9-10.

7 *Financial Times*, 1 October 2000; 'EU - Russia Summit: Joint Declaration', Paris, 30 October 2000 (Brussels: European Commission); Commission of the European Communities, Green Paper, 'Towards a European strategy for the security of energy supplies' (Brussels: COM (2000) 769 final, 29 November 2000), p.87.

8 Commission Green Paper, ibid., p.44.

9 'EU-Russia Summit Joint Statement 3 October 2001', in particular Annex 3 (Brussels: European Commission, October 2001).

10 *Financial Times*, 30 October 2001.

11 Citation from 'Medium-term Strategy for Development of Relations between the Russian Federation and the European Union (2000-2010)', (Brussels: European Commission, 3 November 2000), unofficial translation of 'Strategiya razvitiya otnoshenii Rossiiskoe Federatsii s Evropeiskim Soyuzom na srednesrochnuyu perspektivu (2000-2010 gg.)', *Mezhdunarodnaya Zhizn* 1/2000, pp.40-49.

12 Gowan, op.cit. in n.6, p.22.

13 'Common Strategy of the European Union on Russia', adopted by the European Council in Köln on 4 June 1999 (Brussels: European Commission, 1999/414/CFSP); 'EU-Russia Summit Joint Statement 3 October 2001', op.cit. in n.9.

14 'Medium-term Strategy', op.cit. in n.11.

15 'EU-Russia Summit Joint Statement 3 October 2001', op.cit. in n.9, Annexes 3 and 4.

16 'Common Strategy on Russia', op.cit. in n.13.

17 Solana, 'The EU and Russia Strategic Partnership', op.cit. in n.1; 'Agreement on Partnership and Co-operation', op.cit. in n.5, Article 1.

18 'Council Regulation (EC, Euratom) no.99/2000 of 29 December 1999 concerning the provision of assistance to the partner States in Eastern Europe and Central Asia', *Official Journal L 12*, 18 January 2000, pp.1-9. The development of the aims through the 1990s is traced in 'An evaluation of the Tacis country programme in Russia', Final synthesis report, Volume 1 (henceforth 'Evaluation Report'), undertaken by DRN-Linden for the EC-SCR Evaluation Unit, January 2000, pp.15-16 (available at the EU's Russian delegation website at http://www.eur.ru/eng/tacis/er.htm).

19 'Evaluation Report', ibid., p.ix.

20 See for example Sven Arnswald, *EU Enlargement and the Baltic States: the Incremental Making of New Members* (Helsinki: Finnish Institute for International Affairs and Institut für Europäische Politik, 2000), p.107.

21 'Russian Federation: TACIS Indicative Programme 2000-2003' (available at the Commission's External Relations website http://www.europa.eu.int/comm/external relations/ceeca/tacis/ind act prog.htm), p.16.

22 'The Tacis Programme Annual Report 2000' (Brussels: European Commission, 2001), p.31.

23 Citation from 'Evaluation Report', op.cit. in n.18, p.38.

24 Ibid., pp.xii, 30.

25 Commission of the European Communities, 'Tempus (Phare and Tacis) Annual Report 1998' (Brussels, COM (2000) 455 final, 20 July 2000).

26 Charles Grant, 'How to help Russia', *CEPR Bulletin* Issue 10, February/March 2000 (London: Centre for European Reform).

27 Rodric Braithwaite, *Russia in Europe* (London: Centre for European Reform, 1999), p.47.

28 'Evaluation Report', op.cit. in n.18, pp.44-45.

29 See Table 3.3 on p.85.

30 European Bank for Reconstruction and Development, 'Strategy for the Russian Federation' (London: EBRD, 10 October 2000), p.12.

31 *The Economist*, 24 February 2001.

32 European Bank for Reconstruction and Development, *Transition Report 1999*, cited in *Financial Times*, 9 November 1999.

33 See for example Robert Cottrell, *Financial Times*, 19 September 2001.

34 *Financial Times*, 19 April 2001.

35 'Strategy for the Russian Federation', op.cit. in n.30, p.6.

36 Ibid., pp.5,10.

37 *Financial Times*, 26 September 2000.

38 *Financial Times*, 7 July 2001.

39 'Strategy for the Russian Federation', op.,cit. in n.30, p.5.

40 *Financial Times*, 26 September 2000.

41 'Strategy for the Russian Federation', op.cit. in n.30, pp.25, 26.

42 Ibid., pp.38, 39.

43 Ibid., p.33.

44 Robert Cottrell, 'Putin's Daunting Agenda', *Financial Times*, 13 March 2001, and his 'Movement, if not momentum, in Moscow', *Financial Times*, Survey on Russia, 9 April 2001.

45 'Strategy for the Russian Federation', op.cit. in n.30, p.4.

46 Braithwaite, op.cit. in n.27, p.9.

47 Tommaso Padoa-Schioppa, *Financial and Monetary Integration in Europe: 1990, 1992 and Beyond* (New York and London: Group of Thirty, 1990), p.18.

48 *Financial Times*, 12 July 1990. For the context, see Pinder, op.cit. in n.4, pp.77-79.

49 John Odling-Smee, 'Russia's current economic policies are deserving of support', *IMF Survey*, Vol.28, No.17, 30 August 1999, p.274.

50 'Medium-term Strategy', op.cit. in n.11.

51 See p.48 and The Economist Intelligence Unit, *EIU Country Profile: Russia 2001* (London: EIU, 2001), p.38.

52 Joseph Stiglitz, 'More Instruments and Broader Goals: Moving toward the Post-Washington Consensus', The 1998 WIDER Annual Lecture (Helsinki: January 7, 1998). Stiglitz applied his approach to the case of Russia in 'Whither Reform? Ten Years of Transition', Keynote Address, Annual World Bank Conference on Development Economics, April 28-30, 1999, and in 'Quis custodiet ipsos custodes?', *Challenge*, Nov./Dec., 1999.

53 See Edmond Théry, *La transformation économique de la Russie* (Paris, 1914).

54 M.V. Frunze, the author of Soviet military doctrine, wrote in 1925 that the USSR's forthcoming war with the West would be of a class character. Therefore, 'as a result of a strong military blow to be dealt by us, a class proletarian movement could develop spontaneously in the enemy camp, and the seizure of power by the working class could become possible...', *Voina i Revolyutsia* (*War and Revolution*), (Moscow, May 1925), p.3.

55 *Deloviye Lyudi*, January 1992, p.66.

56 See 'Narodnoye Khozyaistvo SSSR' (The USSR National Economy), (Moscow, 1996), p.671; ibid., 1987, p.647; ibid., 1991, p.651.

57 See S. Sinelnikov, *Budzhetny Krizis v Rossii: 1985-1995 gody* (Budgetary Crisis in Russia: 1985-95), (Moscow: Nauchnaya Kniga, 1995), p.9.

58 'Russian Economic Reform', The World Bank, 1992, p.54.

59 See Yegor Gaidar, *Dni Porazhenii i Pobed* (Days of Defeats and Victories), (Moscow: Wargius, 1996), p.134.

60 Ibid., pp.135-6.

61 'Russian Economic Reform', op.cit. in n.58, p.8.

62 Ibid.

63 *Izvestia*, 6 January 1990.

64 *Nezavisimaya Gazeta*, 4 December 1992.

65 In the second half of the 1980s, private savings in deposits and in cash accounted for 30 per cent of the Soviet Union's GDP, while in 1990 they reached 45 per cent. This predetermined a powerful inflationary outburst after the liberalisation of prices. See 'Russian Economic Reform', op.cit. in n.58, pp.12-13.

66 *European Economy*, No.69 (1999), pp.286-7.

67 See for details Michael Kaser, *Privatisation in the CIS* (London: The Royal Institute of International Affairs, 1995), pp.10-11.

68 Ibid., pp.12, 16.

69 *Dni Porazhenii i Pobed*, op.cit. in n.59, p.92.

70 *Privatisation in the CIS*, op.cit. in n.67, p.15.

71 *Ekonomika Perekhodnogo Perioda. Ocherki Ekonomicheskoi Politiki Perekhodnogo Perioda, 1991-1997* (The Economy in Transition. Essays on Economic Policy of the Transitional Period, 1991-97), (Moscow: IEPP, 1998), pp.438-9. IEPP is Yegor Gaidar's Institute for the Economy in Transition.

72 Ibid., pp.33-4.

73 'Russian Economic Reform', op.cit. in n.58, p.106.

74 *Ekonomika Perekhodnogo Perioda*, op.cit. in n.71, p.504.

75 'Russian Economic Reform', op.cit. in n.58, p.109.

76 'Obzor Ekonomicheskoi Politiki v Rossii za 1999 god' (Review of Russia's Economy for 1999), (Moscow: Economic Analysis Bureau, 2000), pp.338-40.

77 'Narodnoye Khozyaistvo SSSR za 1990 god. Statisticheskii Yezhegodnik' (The USSR National Economy in 1990. Statistical Yearbook), (Moscow: State Statistics Committee, 1991), pp.527-8, 535-6, 543.

78 *Nezavisimaya Gazeta*, 19 February 2000.

79 *Voprosy Statistiki*, 1998, No.9, p.46.

80 Ibid. p.46.

81 Richard Pipes, *Property and Freedom* (New York: Alfred A. Knopf, 1999), p.271.

82 'Bez poter ne oboitis' (We Can't Get by without Losses), *Izvestia*, 12 January 2000.

83 S.V. Pisarevich, 'V Poiskakh Variantov' (In Search of Options), *Nezavisimaya Gazeta*, 20 April 2000.

84 *Rossiiskaya Gazeta*, 16 March 2000.

85 'Rossiya na Rubezhe Vekov' (Russia at the Turn of the Century), An Address by the President of the Russian Federation to the Federal Assembly (Moscow, 1999), p.12.

86 Calculated on the basis of 'Obzor Ekonomicheskoi Politiki', op.cit. in n.76, pp.749, 761.

87 Ibid., p.615.

88 Ibid., p.60.

89 *Russkii Telegraph*, 10 February 1998; *Finansovye Izvestia*, 26 February and 14 October 1998.

90 *Voprosy Statistiki*, 2001, No.5, pp.58, 67.

91 See Yegor Bernstein, 'Kholodnaya Zima 1999 g. posle Goryachego Leta 1998 g. Uroki Avgustovskogo Krizisa' (The Cold Winter of 1999 after the Hot Summer of 1998: Lessons of the August Crisis), *Izvestia*, 18 December 1999.

92 *Voprosy Statistiki*, 2001, No.5, pp.58, 67.

93 *Dni Porazhenii i Pobed*, op.cit. in n.59, p.192.

94 *Izvestia*, 13 March 1999.

95 *Izvestia*, 9 September 1998.

96 *Mirovaya Ekonomika i Mezhdunarodnye Otnosheniya*, 1998, No.8, pp.135, 140, 142; 1999, No.8, p.83.

97 'Summary of Disbursement and Repayments, Russian Federation', IMF, 28 December 2000.

98 *Finansovye Izvestia*, 22 September 1998.

99 *Evropeiskii Soyuz: Fakty i Kommentarii* (European Union: Facts and Comments), No.3 (Moscow, 1996), p.18.

100 Yegor A. Panteleev, *Problemy Torgovykh Otnoshenii Rossii s Evrosoyuzom (1992-1997)*, (Problems Concerning Russia's Trade Relations with the European Union, 1992-97), (Moscow: Nauchnaya Kniga, 1998), pp.55-6.

101 See A. Smith, *Russian Foreign Trade in the Transition* (London: The Royal Institute of International Affairs, 1997), p.33.

102 *Vneshneekonomicheskii Kompleks Rossii: Sostoyaniye i Perspektivy* (Russia's Foreign Economic Complex: State of Affairs and Prospects), (Moscow: VNIKI - All-Russia Market Research Institute, 2000), p.87.

103 *Delovoi Mir*, 19 February and 4-10 October 1997.

104 'Rossiiskaya Ekonomika za 2000 god. Tendentsii i Perspektivy' (Russia's Economy in 2000: Trends and Prospects), (Moscow, 2001), Section 2, p.15.

105 'Inostranniye Investitsii v Rossii' (Foreign Investment in Russia), (Moscow, 1995), pp.436-87.

106 'Rossiiskaya Ekonomika za 2000 god', op.cit. in n.104.

107 *Nezavisimaya Gazeta*, 6 April 2000.

108 *Izvestia*, 24 May 2000.

109 *Vneshneekonomicheskii Kompleks Rossii: Sovremennoye Sostoyaniye i Perspektivy* (Russia's Foreign Economic Complex: Present-Day State of Affairs and Prospects), No. 2 (Moscow: VNIKI - All-Russia Market Research Institute, 1999-2000), p.63; 'Rossiiskaya Ekonomika za 2000 god', op.cit., Section 2.3, pp.5,7.

110 *Ekspert*, 5 November 2001, p.51; *Rossiiskaya biznes-gazeta*, 6 November 2001.

111 Calculated from 'World Investment Report 2000' (New York: UNCTAD, 2000), pp.297-8; *Monthly Bulletin of Statistics*, United Nations, July 2000, pp.2-5.

112 *Indikator*, 1999, No.12, pp.5-6.

113 Calculated on the basis of 'World Investment Report 2000', op.cit. in n.111, Annex table B.1; 'World Development Report 2000' (The World Bank, 2000), pp.296-7.

114 'Obzor Ekonomicheskoi Politiki', op.cit. in n.76, p.378.

115 'Ekonomika Perekhodnogo Perioda', op.cit. in n.71, p.519.

116 'Rossiiskaya Ekonomika v Maye 2001 g.: Tendentsii i Perspektivy' (Russia's Economy in May 2001: Trends and Prospects), (Moscow: IEPP, 2001), p.22.

117 *EIU Country Profile: Russia 2000* (London: The Economist Intelligence Unit, 2000), p.39.

118 *Ekonomika Perekhodnogo Perioda*, op.cit. in n.71, p.492.

119 *Dipkuryer-NG*, No.6, 6 April 2000.

120 Calculated on the basis of Russia's customs statistics, i.e. excluding 'shadow' trade.

121 Here and ff. see I.D. Ivanov, 'Rasshireniye Evrosoyuza: Stsenarii, Problemy i Posledstviya' (The European Union's Enlargement: Scenarios, Problems and Consequences), *Mirovaya Ekonomika i Mezhdunarodniye Otnosheniya*, 1998, No.9, pp.29-32.

122 'EU-Russia Summit Joint Statement 3 October 2001' (Brussels: European Commission, October 2001), Annex 4.

123 'Implementation of the EU/Russia Common Strategy: EU trade policy priorities in the short to medium term' (Brussels: European Commission, 14 September 2000), paragraphs 6 and 19.

124 Michael E. Porter, Jeffrey D. Sachs, Andrew M. Warner, Chris Moore, John M. Tudor, Daniel Vasquez, Klaus Schwab, Peter K. Cornelius, Macha Levinson and Brad Ryder, 'The Global Competitiveness Report 2000' (World Economic Forum: Geneva, 2000), Table 2.

125 'Medium-term Strategy', op.cit. in n.11.

126 Chris Patten and Javier Solana, 'Report on the Western Balkans presented to the Lisbon European Council by the Secretary General/High Representative together with the Commission, 23 March 2000' (Bulletin EU 3-2000, Annex to the Presidency conclusions; SN 2032/2/00 Rev 2).

127 'Nota over de europese politieke unie', Tweede Kamer 1990-1991, 20596, No.32, 26 October 1991, p.24.

128 See Hiski Haukkala, 'The making of the EU's Common Strategy on Russia', in Hiski Haukkala and Sergei Medvedev (eds), *The EU Common Strategy on Russia: Learning the Grammar of the CFSP* (Helsinki: Finnish Institute of International Affairs and Institut für Europäische Politik, 2001), p.34.

129 Stefan De Spiegeleire, 'The Implementation of the EU's Common Strategy on Russia', in Haukkala and Medvedev, ibid., p.104.

130 Richard Holbrook, cited in Quentin Peel, 'Some advice from a friend: time to shape up', *Financial Times*, 17 April 2001.

131 A famous example was the Luxembourg foreign minister's assertion that 'this is the hour of Europe', at the outset of the involvement in the West Balkan wars.

132 'Presidency Conclusions, European Council in Helsinki 10 and 11 December 1999', *Bulletin of the European Union 12-1999*, in particular Annex 4.

133 See Gilles Andréani, Christoph Bertram and Charles Grant, *Europe's Military Revolution* (London: Centre for European Reform, 2001), p.28.

134 'EU-Russia Summit Joint Statement 3 October 2001', op.cit. in n.122, Annex 4.

135 'Common Strategy of the EU on Russia', op.cit. in n.13.

136 Solana, 'The EU and Russia Strategic Partnership', op.cit. in n.1.

137 'EU-Russia Summit Joint Statement 3 October 2001', op.cit. in n.122, Annexes 3 and 4.

138 Haukkala, 'The making of the EU's Common Strategy on Russia', op.cit. in n.128, pp.45-6.

139 'Medium-term Strategy', op.cit. in n.11, pp.40-49.

140 Gowan, *How the EU can help Russia*, op.cit. in n.6, pp.11, 13.

141 Timmermann, *Russlands Strategie*, op.cit. in n.2, pp.9, 31-33.

142 Haukkala, 'The making of the EU's Common Strategy on Russia', op.cit. in n.128, p.53. The impact of the second war in Chechnya on EU-Russia relations is analysed in pp.52-62.

143 Ibid., p.56.

144 Braithwaite, *Russia in Europe*, op.cit. in n.27, p.38.

145 Henry Kissinger, 'The Ill-considered War in Kosovo has Undermined Relations with China and Russia and Put NATO at Risk', *Newsweek*, 31 May 1999, cited in Dusan Sidjanski, *The Federal Future of Europe: From the European Community to the European Union* (Ann Arbor: The University of Michigan Press, 2000), p.394.

146 Joris van Bladel and Stephen Webber, 'Russia's past or future?', *The World Today*, October 2000, p.7.

147 Timmermann, *Russlands Strategie*, op.cit. in n.2, p.17.

148 Stefan Wagstyl, 'Intense suspicion gives way to support', *Financial Times*, Survey on Russia, 9 April 2001.

149 Igor Leshukov, 'Can the Northern Dimension Break the Vicious Circle of Russia-EU Relations?', in Hanna Ojanen (ed.), *The Northern Dimension: Fuel for the EU?* (Helsinki: Finnish Institute for International Affairs and Institut für Europäische Politik, 2001), p.129.

150 See Michael Emerson, et al., *The Elephant and the Bear* (Brussels: Centre for European Policy Studies, 2001).

151 Dmitri Trenin, 'Security Co-operation in North-Eastern Europe: A Russian Perspective', in Dmitri Trenin and Peter van Hamm, *Russia and the United States in North European Security* (Helsinki: Finnish Institute of International Affairs and Institut für Europäische Politik, 2000), p.41.

152 European Parliament, 'The implications of the European Union for co-operation in the field of Justice and Home Affairs', Resolution of 3 April 1998 (OJC No.C138 of 4 May 1998), A4-0107/98, cited in Sven Arnswald, *EU Enlargement and the Baltic States*, op.cit. in n.20, p.143.

153 'Security Co-operation in North-Eastern Europe', op.cit., pp.32-3, 41-2. The author is Deputy Director of the Carnegie Endowment's Moscow Center.

154 Commission of the European Communities, 'Communication on Kaliningrad' (Brussels: European Commission, January 2000); and 'The EU and Kaliningrad', Communication from the Commission to the Council, CCOM (2001) 26 final.

155 Alexander Songal, 'Kaliningrad Oblast: Towards a European Dimension', in James Baxendale, Stephen Dewar and David Gowan (eds), *The EU and Kaliningrad: Kaliningrad and the Impact of Enlargement* (London: The Federal Trust, 2000), p.100.

156 Lyndelle D. Fairlie, 'Kaliningrad Borders in Regional Context', in Lyndelle D. Fairlie and Alexander Sergounin, *Are Borders Barriers? EU Enlargement and the Russian Region of Kaliningrad* (Helsinki: Finnish Institute of International Affairs and Institut für Europäische Politik, 2001), p.10.

157 René Nyberg, 'The Baltic as an Interface between the EU and Russia', in *The EU and Kaliningrad*, op.cit. in n.155, p.55.

158 Alexander Sergounin, 'EU Enlargement and Kaliningrad: The Russian Perspective', in *Are Borders Barriers?*, op.cit. in n.156, p.159.

159 Nyberg, loc.cit. in n.157.

160 Sergounin, 'EU Enlargement and Kaliningrad', op.cit. in n.156, p.150.

161 Ibid., p.150, 159, citing *The Guardian*, 7 April 2001, and *Nezavisimaya Gazeta*, 20 January 2001 and 17 February 2001.

162 Stephen Dewar, 'What is to be done?', in *The EU and Kaliningrad*, op.cit. in n.155, p.259.

163 Ibid., pp.233, 251, 257-60.

164 Chris Patten, 'Preface', in *The EU and Kaliningrad*, op.cit. in n.155, p.7.

165 Emerson, *The Elephant and the Bear*, op.cit. in n.150.

166 Leshukov, 'Can the Northern Dimension Break the Vicious Circle of Russia-EU Relations?', op.cit. in n.149, p.134.

167 Tuomas Forsberg and Hanna Ojanen, 'Finland's new policy: Using the EU for stability in the North', in Gianni Bonvicini, Tapani Vaahtoranta and Wolfgang Wessels (eds), *The Northern EU: National Views on the Emerging Security Dimension* (Helsinki: Finnish Institute of International Affairs and Institut für Europäische Politik, 2000), p.121.

168 *Financial Times*, 5 March 1999, cited in 'Finland's new policy', ibid., pp.119-20.

169 'Action Plan for the Northern Dimension with external and cross-border policies of the European Union 2000-2003', 9400/00, NIS 76 (Brussels: Council of the European Union, 14 June 2000); and 'Presidency Conclusions, European Council in Feira, 19-20 June 2000', *Bulletin of the European Union 6-2000*.

170 Hiski Haukkala, 'National Interests *versus* Solidarity towards Common Policies', in Hanna Ojanen, *The Northern Dimension*, op.cit in n.149, pp.113-14.

171 International Panel on Climate Change Working Group 1, *Third Assessment Report*, January 2001 (http://www/meto/gov.uk/sec5/CR div/ipcc/wg1/ipcctar.html).

172 For the latter, see the Ministry of Defence report, 'The future strategic context for defence', (http://www.mod.gov.uk), cited in Hermann E. Ott, 'Climate change: an important foreign policy issue', *International Affairs*, Vol.77, No.2, April 2001, p.295.

173 Ott, ibid., p.290.

174 Cited in Aubrey Meyer, *Contraction and Convergence: The Global Solution to Climate Change* (Dartington, Devon: Green Books on behalf of The Schumacher Society, 2000), p.92. See also Michael Grubb and Farhana Yamin, 'Climatic collapse at The Hague: what happened, why, and where do we go from here?', *International Affairs*, Vol.77, No.2, April 2001, p.262.

175 *Financial Times*, 12 June 2001; Royal Commission on Environmental Pollution, *Energy – The Changing Climate*, Cm 4794 (London: Her Majesty's Stationery Office, June 2000).

176 Arild Moe and Kristian Tangen, *The Kyoto Mechanisms and Russian Climate Politics* (London: The Royal Institute of International Affairs, 2000), pp.99-101; Benito Miller, *Ratifying the Kyoto Protocol: The case for Japanese-Russian joint implementation*, Briefing Paper New Series No.21 (London: The Royal Institute of International Affairs, May 2001), p.4.

177 Ott, 'Climate change', op.cit. in n.172, p.283.

178 See Grubb and Yamin, 'Climatic collapse at The Hague', op.cit. in n.174, p.273, with citation from conference address of the Head of the Russian delegation on 21 November 2000.

179 Ibid., pp.274-5.

180 Ott, 'Climate change', op.cit. in n.172, p.295.

181 See Christopher Layton, *A Climate Community: A European Initiative with the South*, European Essay No.15 (London: The Federal Trust, 2001).

182 'Rossiya i Evropa na rubezhe stoletii', *Mezhdunarodnaya Zhizn*, 2/2000, pp.24-29, cited in Timmermann, *Russlands Strategie*, op.cit. in n.2, pp.30-31.

183 See for example Gwyn Prins (ed.), *Understanding Unilateralism in American Foreign Relations* (London: The Royal Institute of International Affairs, 2000).

184 *The Independent*, 15 January 2001; *Financial Times*, 9 April 2001; *The Economist*, 3 March 2001.

185 Tony Blair, speech delivered in Warsaw in October 2000, reprinted as *Superpower - not Superstate?*, European Essay No.12 (London: The Federal Trust, 2000), p.18.

186 Chris Patten, 'A European Foreign Policy: Ambition and Reality', speech delivered in Paris to the Institut Français des Relations Internationales, 15 June 2000.

187 Ibid.

188 Samuel P. Huntington, 'The lonely superpower', *Foreign Affairs*, March-April 1999, p.48.

189 EU-Russia Summit Joint Statement 3 October 2001, op.cit. in n.9.

190 Matthias Jopp, 'Introduction', in Mathias Jopp and Riku Warjovaara (eds), *Approaching the Northern Dimension of the CFSP: Challenges and opportunities for the EU in the emerging European security order* (Helsinki: Finnish Institute of International Affairs and Institut für Europäische Politik, 1998), p.23.

191 Dmitri Trenin, 'A Russian Perspective', in Trenin and van Hamm, *Russia and the United States*, op.cit. in n.151, pp.39-40; Lawrence Freedman, 'The transformation of Nato', *Financial Times*, 6 August 2001.

192 Richard Holbrook, cited in Quentin Peel, 'Some advice from a friend: time to shape up', *Financial Times*, 17 April 2001.

193 Chris Patten, 'A European Foreign Policy', op.cit. in n.186.

194 Gowan, *How the EU can help Russia*, op.cit. in n.6, pp.6, 30.

195 Jack Straw, Secretary of State for Foreign Affairs, speech at The Royal Institute of International Affairs, 27 July 2001.

196 Solana, 'The EU and Russian strategic partnership', op.cit. in n.1.